GUARDING THE ROCK

GUARDING THE ROCK
A Father and Son Remember Alcatraz

Ernest B. Lageson, Sr.
and
Ernest B. Lageson

GOLDEN GATE NATIONAL PARKS CONSERVANCY
SAN FRANCISCO, CALIFORNIA

Library of Congress Control Number 2008925258
ISBN 978-1-932519-04-4

Photographs included in this book are from a number of sources, and may be protected by copyright or have other use restrictions. For use-related questions, please contact the relevant individual or archive.

Front cover: John Louie.

Courtesy of the Golden Gate NRA, Park Archives: Betty Wallar Photo Collection: pp. 13 GOGA 19200.318, 26 (bottom) GOGA 19200.249, 27 (top left, top to bottom right) GOGA 19200.263, GOGA 19200.242, GOGA 19200.200, GOGA 19200, 49 (top) GOGA 19200.120, 62 (bottom) GOGA 19200, 63 (top) GOGA 19200.268; Sheppeard Alcatraz Collection: p. 62 (bottom) GOGA 40046.049; Alcatraz 1946 Riot Photo Collection GOGA 18341.19 © E. E. Waller: p. 15; Jon A. Peters Alcatraz Collection GOGA35266.016: p. 25; Alcatraz Penitentiary Photos: p. 27 (bottom left) GOGA 17019; Associated Press: pp. 28 (top left), 85 (top); Charles Berta Alcatraz Photos: p. 28 (top right) GOGA 17588; Weed/McPherson Alcatraz Papers GOGA 35178: pp. 41, 44, 45 (top), 50 (middle); Chandler/Bates Alcatraz Photo Album: p. 45 (bottom) GOGA 40017; Henry Family Alcatraz Photos: p. 48 (bottom) GOGA 40023; DeNevi Alcatraz Photos: p. 87 (top left) GOGA 18261; Maurice Ordway Papers: p. 114 (top) GOGA 35335.25; p. 166 GOGA 2316 Interp Neg Collection #80-C-198

Courtesy of the San Francisco Public Library: pp. 125 (left), 168 (top left); Acme Photo: p. 166 (top right).

Courtesy of the Federal Bureau of Prisons, NARA-Pacific Region: All prisoner mug shots

Other photographs courtesy of Ernest B. Lageson Collection; Estate of Emil and Beatrice Rychner; Chuck Stucker Collection.

Cover and text design by Ernie Lageson III.

Produced through the Interpretive Media Division of the Golden Gate National Parks Conservancy: Robert Lieber and Sarah Lau, with technical assistance from Vivian Young and Susan Tasaki

Printed in the USA

The Golden Gate National Parks Conservancy is the nonprofit membership organization created to preserve the Golden Gate National Parks, enhance the experiences of park visitors, and build a community dedicated to conserving the parks for the future.

Visit *www.parksconservancy.org and www.nps.gov/alcatraz.*

TABLE OF CONTENTS

Preface

Guarding the Rock is by, about, and in honor of my father, Ernest B. Lageson, Sr.

Dad was an educator by profession, but for approximately four years in the 1940s he worked as a correctional officer at the United States Penitentiary, Alcatraz Island. During part of that time, our family lived on the island as members of the community of approximately 300 prison employees and their families who called The Rock their home.

Life on Alcatraz was, at various times, normal, unusual, fascinating, bizarre, and even dull. Dad's brief tenure as a prison guard included all of the above as well as the spectacular and the terrifying. In May 1946, he was one of nine men taken hostage during the bloodiest and most sensational escape attempt in the history of the island prison. Before order was restored, the two-day uprising claimed the lives of two officers and three inmates. Fifteen officers, including Dad, and one prisoner were wounded during the murderous gunfire.

Although Dad had decided well before the 1946 breakout attempt to leave prison work and return to education, he stayed on at Alcatraz until after the murder trial of the surviving inmates, who were charged with killing one of the hostages. His trial testimony was instrumental in the conviction of the three defendants, two of whom received the death penalty for their crimes. In part because of Dad's testimony, the jury spared the life of the third inmate, Clarence Carnes, and sentenced him to life in prison.

During the early 1950s, at my urging, Dad began writing a book about his experiences on Alcatraz. His untimely death in 1953 ended his literary career before it had really begun. When he died, I was a twenty-year-old college senior, and I promised myself that someday I would write a book that told the story of his 1946 experiences, which fate had prevented him from doing. My demanding career as a civil trial lawyer kept me from making good on that promise until I retired from active law practice. In 1999, *Battle at Alcatraz* was published telling the story of the

1946 escape attempt, and in 2002, *Alcatraz Justice* was released, describing the murder trial of the three surviving inmates. The first book was dedicated to Dad, and together, the two books memorialized the entire 1946 story, I hope the way Dad would have wanted it told.

I always felt that Dad's original manuscript deserved publication, and now I have seen to that. I edited, updated, and added to his original work to produce *Guarding the Rock, A Father and Son Remember Alcatraz*. Once again, I hope he would be pleased with the work. It was a labor of love for me, and I am proud to have co-authored a book with my father, a man for whom I have always had great love and respect.

To enhance the readers' enjoyment and understanding, the book contains numerous photographs. Many of these are family pictures or photos I took myself. Several of the photographs were supplied by my friend and fellow former "child of Alcatraz," Chuck Stucker, and I thank him profusely for his generous support. Other pictures in the book came to me from Michael Esslinger, the author of an out-standing book about Alcatraz, *Alcatraz, A Definitive History of the Penitentiary Years*, and our good friends Emil Rychner, ("Rych"), a former captain of the guard, and his wife Bea. Rych worked as an Alcatraz correctional officer in various capacities from 1935 to 1961, and saw virtually all of what is today the history of The Rock.

Finally, I would like to acknowledge and thank with great pride my son Ernie III for his work in designing the cover of the book. His creative contribution makes this a three-generation work.

Ernest B. Lageson

Prologue

I looked in horror at the five other prison officers with me in cell #403 who had just been shot. None of them moved; I feared they were all dead. Sam Shockley, one of the would-be escapees, pointed down at me.

"Hey, Joe! There's a son-of-a-bitch in the corner that's still alive. Kill him."

Joe Cretzer, a convict I'd had several friendly discussions with over the years, tried to shrug off the command.

"Naw, that's Mr. Lageson. He's a good guy and always treated me right. He's my friend."

"Friend, hell!" Miran Thompson, another convict yelled. "He'll testify against us. He'll go to court and screw us all. Kill him!"

Joe glanced nervously at the others. They were all watching him.

"If you don't wanna kill him, Joe, then gimme the goddam gun and I will," Thompson said.

Joe hesitated, and looked down at me with regret. "Mr. Lageson, I'm really sorry about this," he said almost in a whisper.

He aimed the gun at me, right at my face.

I asked God to look after my wife, Eunice, and little Ernie, our son. Please keep them safe. I waited to die, thinking back in a swirl of memories. Back to where life for me had begun.

It seemed so very long ago.

Chapter I

From North Dakota to Alcatraz

"Son, if you're not careful, you'll wind up in a penitentiary." Grave and somber words. Little did the speaker realize how oddly clairvoyant they were. I recall my father uttering that phrase as he chastised me for some youthful misdemeanor during my austere upbringing in the northernmost reaches of North Dakota. It was a harsh and challenging part of the country, populated by strong, dedicated immigrants determined to make a better life than they had known in Europe.

Not much of significance happened to a boy in the early twentieth century who lived in Sharon, a North Dakota village of three hundred and sixty-five inhabitants. The town was located on the edge of the Red River Valley, approximately one hundred miles north of Fargo, the "metropolis" of North Dakota. I attended the public elementary and high schools, both of which were located in the same building, so we had the rather tedious prospect of our entire general education being in the same location. My father was the custodian of the school. He also served as town marshall, whose principal duties were maintaining order Saturday night on Main Street when the farm boys were in town. This job was made somewhat easier by the fact that Dad also ran the pool hall, the only alcohol-dispensing institution in town.

After graduation from high school in 1927, I eschewed farm life in favor of higher education, and attended Concordia College in Moorhead, Minnesota. A small Lutheran college, Concordia was endowed by the Norwegian Lutheran Church of America. My years at Concordia were during the hectic Prohibition Era, and though somewhat wild, were much the same as in any small college town at the time.

I graduated from Concordia in 1931 with a Bachelor of Arts degree and a major in biology, prepared to teach that subject to young high school America. During my first year as a high school instructor in Kloten, North Dakota, I met the girl who was later to become my wife. Eunice McLean was the primary teacher in the local school, where I extended my first efforts at imparting knowledge to unwilling adolescent minds.

During the ensuing years, my career as an educator took me to several North Dakota communities, where I served in various capacities as part of the state public school system. At Zion, a small community near the larger town of Cando, I aided the residents by founding a two-year high school. It was 1933, the heart of the Depression, and the local farmers appreciated the opportunity to keep the boys and girls on the farm for two more years before they traveled to Cando to complete their high school education. The locality was made up predominately of members of the Church of the Brethren, commonly called Dunkers, for their custom of baptismal immersion. The community fathers advised in no uncertain terms (as stated in my contract) that I was to refrain from the use of alcohol and tobacco. In this rural school, I labored as the principal, administrator, teacher, secretary, and janitor. Many were the North Dakota winter mornings when the thermometer stood at thirty degrees below zero, and the school was not fully warm until noon. All this was done for the princely salary of fifty-five dollars per month for the nine-month school year. I was not paid during the summer months, so had to find alternate sources of income.

During our three-year sojourn at Zion, we were particularly fortunate to obtain accommodations with a couple of bachelor farm brothers, Joseph and Frank Denny, just a half a mile from the school. Due to the lack of housing in the area, we were thankful to be taken in by these fine young men. We lived with the Denny brothers through three bitter winters, Eunice doing the cooking and housework, and I, to the extent my time permitted, helping about the farm. The Dennys furnished the milk and the meat and we split the cost of groceries and coal. Despite our meager income during the years in Zion, we were able to purchase a secondhand 1929 Ford sedan and a gasoline-powered Maytag washer. Unfortunately, the washer could not be used in the house because of the exhaust, so clothes washing was an outdoor activity even during the frigid North Dakota winters. Our son Ernie Jr., born in 1932, shared a folding day bed with Eunice and me during those long winter nights. The Round Oak heater stoked with North Dakota lignite coal could barely produce enough heat to warm the ancient farmhouse.

The board of education at Zion was pleased with my performance, and for two successive years, I was given a ten-dollar per month raise in salary. The fourth year, the board saw fit to increase the salary by only five dollars per month. In explaining his position regarding the humble salary increase, one of the members said, "Five dollars will give Lageson quite a bit to run his car on."

Unimpressed with the board's generosity, I searched for alternative employment and learned of a vacancy in a small consolidated school in the village of Hansboro. This tiny hamlet was situated just three miles from the Canadian border, and was a port of entry into the province of Manitoba. Here the principalship paid the handsome salary of a hundred dollars per month, and carried considerably more prestige. In Hansboro, the principal had supervision over a combined four-year high school and eight-year elementary school employing four teachers. After a number of interviews, I was selected for the job from a large field of applicants. The family proceeded at once to Devils Lake, where we established credit at the local Montgomery Ward store, and we spent lavishly (for us), outfitting the house we had rented in Hansboro. We bought furniture, curtains, linoleum (we couldn't afford carpets), and accessories, running up a bill in excess of a thousand dollars.

Unfortunately, we were denied the house of our choice because the owner was unable to evict the existing tenants. The occupant was "on relief," the 1930s equivalent of welfare, and his "relief" status protected him from eviction. There was nothing anyone could do to move him out. In addition, he had nowhere to go. After a couple of months battling houseflies and the summer heat in an old harvest cook car, which a kind citizen had permitted us to use, we moved into a lovely home with a local widower, Mr. Charles E. Blackorby. Charlie, the town banker, lived alone with his son, Stuart, a sophomore in high school. We spent two very happy years with the Blackorbys, and in 1938, we were finally able to rent a place of our own.

But that proved to be our last year in Hansboro. During the first semester, I had seen fit to chastise the unruly children of two members of the three-member school board. The son of one board member was corrected for some misconduct, then chose to withdraw from school. His father told the boy he could return to school the following year, because by then, Lageson would be gone. The young lad never did return to school.

The daughter of another board member adopted the attitude that her father's position in the community placed her above the rest of the student body when it came to work performance and adherence to school rules. When her demeanor and conduct repeatedly failed to conform to established rules, she was expelled. Her father, unfortunately, viewed his daughter as the blameless victim of an erring principal, who needed to be taught a lesson.

The third member of the board was kind enough to advise me that my days were numbered. Pursuant to his suggestion, I initiated a job search, and once more we were on the march. This time it led to the small community of Clyde, where we spent three very happy years. The school was the same size as Hansboro, but the overall conditions were infinitely better.

The educational system that existed in the rural communities of the Midwestern states in the 1930s was a far cry from the schools of today. Schools in the larger towns had two or three elementary grade teachers with two to four grades in each room. The high school faculty usually consisted of one teacher in addition to the principal, who was also an instructor. Generally, all the grades were housed in one building. It was the duty of the principal to supervise both the elementary and secondary schools. In addition, he performed a myriad of other duties and responsibilities, including administering all state and standard testing programs, coaching the athletic teams, directing dramatic productions, supervising the school paper and yearbook, handling all problems of discipline, attending to all employment matters, and answering to the whims of the school board, none of the members of which customarily had any knowledge of educational matters. Also, he generally taught three to five classes of high school subjects per day. The thirties and early forties were very difficult times for school personnel in most districts of North Dakota. The droughts and the Great Depression made the supply of dollars meager. Taxes for school purposes were difficult and sometimes impossible to collect, and the salaries of

Kloten, ND, where Eunice and Ernest met.

The Kloten school where Eunice taught in the elementary grades and Ernest taught in the high school.

The Clyde, ND, school where Ernest served as, among other things, superintendent, principal, and high school teacher, and Eunice taught in the elementory grades. Young Ernie attended second through fourth grades, and in the fourth grade his mother was his teacher.

Ernest, Eunice, and young Ernie with new 1941 Ford. It was the first new car the Lageson family ever had.

teachers and other school people were low. At times, school personnel could not even cash the warrants issued by the school districts.

Since school employees were only paid for the nine months school was in session, a great many of the male employees spent their summers selling encyclopedias or aluminum cookware door-to-door, or working on local farms. In our case, we were blessed with employment during the harvest on Eunice's father's nearby farm. I worked as a field hand, and Eunice worked as a cook preparing meals for the twenty or more temporary farm workers hired to harvest the various crops. The female teachers were more limited in jobs available to them, but they too had to find alternate forms of income. School employees faced a complete lack of job security. School boards would often inform teachers at the end of the school year that their contracts were not being renewed for the coming year. No reason needed. Most men in the educational field with families to support were constantly searching for added sources of income.

Eunice and I had considered various other employment options, and had examined the possibility of employment within the federal Civil Service system. I took the employment examinations of several federal agencies, including the Departments of Justice, Treasury, and Labor. I was tentatively selected for employment as an immigration officer, but was rejected because I was an eighth of an inch below the minimum height requirement.

But then came a letter from the Department of Justice, Bureau of Prisons. I had successfully passed the test for junior custodial officer, and the bureau wanted to know if I was available for appointment. *Was I available?* We posted a response letter within an hour informing the bureau "I was ready for appointment!" And the wait began.

It was a bright June morning shortly after the end of the 1941–42 school year, and I was puttering about the garden (we raised all our own vegetables in a huge garden). Frank Batemen, chairman of the local school board, drove up and asked if I was interested in accompanying him to a farm sale. Frank was building his herd of cattle and was interested in purchasing a couple of young heifers. I agreed to go along, and we drove fifteen or twenty miles to a sale in the nearby town of Egeland. We spent most of the day at the sale and arrived back at Clyde in the late afternoon. As we stopped in front of the house, Eunice came running toward us, flushed with excitement, waving a letter.

"Ernie, Ernie, we're going to Alcatraz!"

Alcatraz, America's Devil's Island, situated in the middle of San Francisco Bay! It was the home of such notorious bad men as George "Machine Gun" Kelly and Alvin "Creepy" Karpis, and the former home of the most famous gangster of the times, Al "Scarface" Capone. Could this be possible? What a switch, from the quiet solitude of the North Dakota prairie and the kindly farm folk of middle America. What sort of life would this be?"

"Gee, Ernie," Frank said incredulously, "do you really think you'd want to go there?"

"I don't know. We'll have to think about it."

"The salary is $1,860 dollars a year, honey," Eunice said, "and they want you out there in just a few days."

The financial impact was huge. The salary was almost double what I was earning, even considering the raise Frank told me the board would be giving me. Living expenses would probably be higher, but in California there'd be no more blizzards, muddy roads, or enormous coal bills. We wouldn't have to grow and can our own vegetables, and we'd have indoor plumbing. No more using an outhouse in below-zero weather. There would also be the security of a year 'round paycheck from the federal government with all the accompanying employee benefits. It was an economic bonanza.

"Wow, Frank!" I said, "we'll have to think this over pretty carefully."

"Well, let me know what you intend to do. This is obviously a big decision, and I have no desire to rush you. Rest assured, the board will delay any contract discussions until you make up your mind. We don't want to lose you, but we want you to make the right decision for you and your family."

Once alone, Eunice and I reviewed the magnitude of such a move: working in a prison containing the incorrigible prisoners of the federal prison system. What did I know about being a prison guard? It was an island in the middle of San Francisco Bay and the obvious target in the event of a Japanese bombing attack on the West Coast similar to the one at Pearl Harbor. But despite the unknowns and the potential dangers, the opportunity was too great to pass up. I could give Alcatraz a try for a month or so, and if it didn't work out, probably return to my job at Clyde. If Clyde wouldn't hold my job, and Alcatraz didn't work out, I could return to teaching in California.

A day later, we drove our shiny new 1941 Ford to Devils Lake, where I entrained on the crack Empire Builder, the finest rolling stock of the Great Northern Railway. There was no Pullman space available as it was all reserved for military and other government personnel, so I rode day coach to San Francisco. The next Sunday was Father's Day, and Ernie presented me with my Father's Day gift early, a box of candy with a pipe taped to the box.

On Sunday, June 21, 1942, I stepped off the train at the underground rail station in Oakland, California, and took the ferry across the bay to San Francisco. As we crossed the bay, I stood on the upper deck, awed by the view of the harbor, the islands, the bridges, the skyline, and Alcatraz. There she lay, surmounted by a halo (or would it be a pall) of fog, silent and forbidding like a ghost ship at anchor. The scene was at once beautiful and sinister. What awaited me on The Rock? What would this new life be like?

I stepped off the ferry and walked quickly through the Ferry Building to gaze at bustling Market Street, the city's main thoroughfare. Since it was Sunday, I assumed everything would be quiet, but Market Street was teeming with auto, pedestrian, and streetcar traffic. It was like nothing I'd ever seen, and I was overwhelmed by the thought of being a country bumpkin in the middle of a huge city as I stood there in my lightweight summer suit and black-and-white shoes facing the howling wind of the San Francisco summer. In my inside breast pocket was my letter of introduction from the Bureau of Prisons, my passport to The Rock.

Quickly focusing on my mission, I realized I had to get to Alcatraz, but had no idea how to do that. Spotting the Ferry Building Police Station, I walked in and inquired how I might get to the island. None of the police officers in the substation had the faintest idea of how to get to Alcatraz. One enterprising officer, however, telephoned the island and spoke to the man in the armory. He said that I should take one of the streetcars running on Market Street that crossed Van Ness Avenue. At Van Ness, I was to transfer to the H car and ride it to the end of the line. Thereafter I was to walk to Army Pier 4 at the foot of Van Ness and board the boat to Alcatraz, being careful not to get on the boat to Angel Island, which also used Pier 4. The policeman seemed tentative and unsure of the directions, leaving me something less than confident regarding the route. He also warned that some of the areas in that section of town were under tight military control and off-limits to the general public.

To simplify matters, I hailed a passing Yellow Cab. "Take me to Pier 4 at the foot of Van Ness Avenue, where I can catch the launch to Alcatraz." The cabby drove along the waterfront rather than Van Ness Avenue as suggested by the Alcatraz armory officer. As I had been warned, the route went through restricted areas and military police posts were located all along the way. At our first checkpoint as we drove along the Embarcadero, I produced my letter signed by Warden Johnston naming me as a junior custodial officer and authorizing my transportation to the island. At each subsequent checkpoint, the driver announced, "Show him the letter," and each military policeman passed us through.

Eventually, we arrived at Pier 4, where I stood with a suitcase in each hand gazing at the island that was to become such a large part of us, and we a small part of it.

Chapter II

The Training Period

As I waited for the boat, I observed those who were obviously members of the Alcatraz custodial force and their families talking of their activities of the day, those to come, and family matters. They all seemed pretty normal even though they were from Alcatraz. The dock was manned by military personnel headed by a master sergeant, who was in full command of what was going on. A large ferryboat, the *General Frank M. Coxe*, was tied up at the pier, which I quickly identified as the boat to Fort McDowell on Angel Island. The Alcatraz motor launch, also known as the *McDowell* would arrive at 3:45 p.m. I didn't feel comfortable introducing myself to the assembled group, so I loitered about the pier until the *McDowell* put in at the small floating dock secured to the east end of Pier 4. As I stepped onto the float, a prison officer inquired as to my identity and I once again displayed the all-important letter.

"Oh," he said expectantly, "you're the new officer arriving today. Welcome aboard."

My, I thought, *they're expecting me. How grand to be so well received.*

I boarded the launch with some apprehension since the largest water craft I'd ever been on was a rowboat on one of North Dakota's few lakes. The lines were tossed off and we headed for The Rock. The ten-minute voyage was uneventful and before I knew it, we were grinding full astern and gliding into the slip at the island dock.

After the women and children disembarked, I was escorted to the dock office by the boat officer, Maurice Ordway, and introduced to Dock Lieutenant Ike Faulk. I signed an identification form and was whisked, in a small bus, up to the cellhouse located on the top level of the island. In the cellhouse office area, I met the administrative staff and the associate warden, Edward J. Miller. Miller's easy manner immediately put me at ease.

"Well, Ernie, let's get you on the roster right away so you can start drawing your pay."

"That's fine with me," I happily responded as I followed the associate warden into his office.

During this initial period of introductions and small talk, I made a quick survey of my surroundings. Nothing too different from any other office area, I thought, except for the glass and steel box in one corner of the captain's office. This small enclosure was about fifteen by seven feet, and there seemed to be no opening to it except a small wicket about a foot and a half square. Inside the sinister-looking little cage was an officer cleaning a pistol, occasionally answering the phone, and periodically issuing keys and weapons to officers through the small wicket. This was the armory, the veritable nerve center of the island and the prison. Here were stored and maintained all the firearms on Alcatraz. It was also the communications and information center of the prison and contained one of the two telephone lines to the outside world. The other line was a pay phone in the office area. The paper work required to process me from Ernest B. Lageson, schoolteacher, to Ernest B. Lageson, junior custodial officer, did not take long.

The administrative details complete, I was assigned a room in the bachelor officer's quarters and notified to appear the next morning to receive my uniforms and shoes. I strolled back down the hill to my new quarters, admiring the breathtaking view of San Francisco, the Golden Gate Bridge, and the hills surrounding the bay. The door to my room, like all the doors in the BOQ, was not locked and I was issued no key. I later learned that none of the residences on the island were locked. This came as no particular surprise, since no one locked their doors in Clyde, and unlocked doors were a generally accepted social practice of the times. My room was the quintessential institutional domicile, sterile and sparsely furnished. It was basic living, only a cut above the quarters of the men I was here to guard, and could best be described as depressing.

That evening, I was taken in tow by one of the other bachelors, who sug-

Officers receiving training in hand-to-hand combat during the indoctrination period.

gested that we go to dinner together. Happy for the company, I readily accepted his offer and we climbed the hill to the officers' mess in the cellhouse. As we entered the main cell block area, I was nervous and apprehensive. We proceeded through the main gate sally port and into the cellhouse. We walked down Broadway, the name given the main corridor through the cellhouse. The intersecting corridor at the end of Broadway was referred to as Times Square because of the large clock mounted on the west gun gallery in that corridor. As we walked down Broadway, I was immediately aware of being under the intense scrutiny of dozens of men locked in very small cells. None of them spoke; they just stared at me. Not yet ready to make eye contact with any of them, I looked straight ahead as we walked. We passed through Times Square, then the prisoners' mess hall and into the officers' mess. The officer's mess was a small room just off the kitchen, separated from the inmate mess hall by bars and a heavy gate.

My apprehension increased as time went on, for here we were locked in the kitchen with approximately twenty dangerous criminals, and just outside the kitchen were some two hundred and fifty more. Although it looked forboding to me at first, I was able to allay my concern somewhat by telling myself, "This is how it's done in prison, and apparently the system works."

Ambling down the hill to my room after dinner, I was conscious of the brisk wind blowing through the Golden Gate and the bank of fog lying offshore. I shivered perceptibly. The chill June winds of Alcatraz were a far cry from the balmy spring evenings in North Dakota. Upon reaching my quarters, I penned a letter to the folks back in Clyde, giving them the highlights of the trip and my new island life. That letter, and several that followed, were anything but upbeat. It was the first time that our little family had ever been separated, and I was just plain lonesome. I didn't know if I was going to like this business of being a prison guard. It occurred to me that perhaps I should go back to Clyde, take that raise in pay and continue on as a small town school superintendent. Then I thought of our nine-year-old son, Ernie Jr., who was dreaming of his new life in California and could think of little else. "No," I said to myself, "you'd better stick this thing out for at least a couple months. It can't possibly be as bad as it looks right now." Exhausted from the long trip and the tension of the new and sinister-seeming surroundings, I quickly fell asleep. After only a few hours, however, the unfamiliar moan of the foghorns roused me. Unable to get back to sleep, I got up, lit a cigarette, and went to the window. Heavy fog shrouded the island, blotting out the light from the moon, stars, and mainland. It was a foreboding feeling, which only deepened my sense of loneliness and gloom.

I felt better in the morning, and went about the business of drawing my uniforms. Each probationary officer was issued two uniform jackets, with four pairs of trousers, a heavy melton cloth overcoat, two pairs of black oxfords, a rubber raincoat of the type typically worn by police officers, and cap with a badge bearing the insignia of the federal Bureau of Prisons. I was also issued a badge, which was to be worn in the jacket lapel. I was instructed that this badge was to be worn backwards and under the lapel, with only the button on the backside of the badge showing through the buttonhole. An old timer later told me that initially the badge, in the shape of a shield, was worn on the jacket lapel so it was visible like that on a police officer's uniform. Apparently someone in the bureau's Washington, D. C., office felt the badge was too authoritarian, and directed that they be concealed. Why the inmates at Alcatraz needed to be sheltered from the authoritarianism of a badge was

Fire drill using the Alcatraz fire engine. The Alcatraz fire department was made up entirely of custodial officers who lived on the island.

a question that defied answer. Authority dominated every minute of their lives, so how did hiding a badge change anything? But I placed the badge backward in my lapel and reported to Associate Warden Miller's office, where I was duly sworn in as a custodial officer of the Bureau of Prisons. Like the rest of us, Associate Warden Miller's badge was also hidden from view.

The issue of clothing and other administrative details consumed the entire morning, so I went with several other officers to the mess hall for lunch. Once again we were locked into our little room while we and the main body of prisoners ate the noon meal. After lunch I was sent down to the dock, where I spent the rest of the day observing the work of the officers and inmates in what was one of the busiest venues on the island. It was my first exposure to actual prison work, and I thoroughly enjoyed it.

The dock was the focal point of island activity, since everything coming to or leaving the island passed through it. Two small ships, the *El Aquador* and the *El Acquario*, serviced the supply needs of Alcatraz, and one or the other of the ships was moored to the dock almost continuously. The ships, known to the island residents as "the water boats," annually brought millions of gallons of fresh water to the island for industrial and personal use. The water was stored in a huge elevated tank at the northwest end of the island. But the little tankers were cargo ships as well, and brought to the island all the food, industrial materials, and supplies of every kind for the prison. All this freight was unloaded and moved about the island by convict labor. Approximately fifteen inmates worked on the dock.

Much of the work performed on the dock was related to the war effort. The largest prison industry was the laundry, and millions of tons of laundry from military installations around the Bay Area were done on the island. Huge bags of laundry were moved from the two small water tankers to the dock by steam winches and loaded onto large carts. Inmates pushed these carts to a covered area on the dock, where the soiled material was searched for contraband before being trucked to the laundry. The processing of the incoming laundry was an enormous and tedious job. Every bag was opened, the laundry emptied upon a long table and given a thorough search ("shakedown"). The dock officers did the actual searching while the inmates emptied the contents of the bags and filled them after the search. The bags were then loaded on trucks and hauled to the laundry located in the prison industries building at the northwest end of the island. Another wartime activity on the dock was sandblasting, repairing, and repainting the buoys that supported the anti-submarine net stretched across the Golden Gate. The buoys were carried by Coast Guard barges to and from Alcatraz, and the work was performed by the inmates.

The prison garage was located at the dock, and here the trucks and the bus were serviced and repaired. One inmate was assigned as mechanic, and it was his job, under the supervision of the truck officer, to keep the rolling stock in working order. It was a highly desirable job for any inmate qualified to do the work.

The dock was under the supervision of a lieutenant, who had four officers to assist in the various activities. In addition to the lieutenant, there was the dock officer, truck officer, laundry shakedown officer, and delivery officer. The dock officer's duties included riding the island motor launch on its regular runs to the mainland. The truck officer was in charge of all the motor vehicles, four pick-up trucks and the small passenger bus. The delivery officer, with inmate assistance, delivered milk, laundry, and dry cleaning to the homes and apartments of the custodial and administrative personnel living on the island. The laundry shakedown officer had the most difficult job, searching all the incoming laundry. This responsibility usually went to the junior officer on the dock crew, but there was a small compensation. Military uniforms comprised much of the laundry and uniform pockets frequently yielded items of value. Although efforts were made to return items to the owners, this was rarely possible, and usually the searching officer got to keep what he found.

In addition to the close personal supervision the inmates received on the dock, they were under the constant surveillance of the armed officer above them in the dock tower. This man had a vantage point about fifty feet above the dock in a glass-enclosed tower with a surrounding catwalk. He was armed with a .30 caliber rifle, a Thompson submachine gun, and a .45 caliber automatic pistol. Entrance to the tower was through a trap door in the floor, accessible after ascending a circular stairway through a locked gate in a high cyclone and barbed wire fence at the base of the tower. The dock tower was also the repository of the key to the motor launch. Except when the boat was in use, the key was in the tower safely out of the reach of any inmate with escape on his mind. Over the years, I had many job assignments on the island, but my favorite work venue was the dock. There was constant activity and excitement, the officers and inmates worked hard, and there was a camaraderie there that didn't exist at any of the other work sites.

My second day of indoctrination was under the tutelage of the officer in charge of the cellhouse. For the first time, I came face-to-face with the prison's general population of approximately 250 inmates whom the federal prison system had determined to be incorrigible in other institutions. These men occupied B and C cell blocks. There were another twenty-five or thirty prisoners in D Block, the isolation section of the prison, men whom the Alcatraz administration considered the "incorrigibles among the incorrigibles." These men were considered so dangerous or difficult to control that they were confined to their cells virtually twenty-four hours a day. Their meals were served to them in their cells, and they were released from their cells only for brief exercise periods of an hour or two a week and a weekly shower.

By far the tensest time in the cellhouse was during the mass movement of the inmates. During passage to and from meals, to and from work, and to and from the recreation yard, 250 violent criminals moved freely through the cellhouse under the supervision of only a handful of unarmed custodial officers. This mass movement occurred ten times a day, 365 days a year. Assuming an average of 250 inmates in general population, that computed to nearly a million opportunities for violence during those movements.

I spent much of the second morning learning the operation of the locking mechanism located at the end of each tier of cells. This device was so constructed that an officer could open or close one, some, or all the cells in a bank of fifteen. It was a mechanical arrangement consisting of various levers, and by the end of the morning I had mastered the procedure.

After the noon meal, I was exposed to another phase of the shakedown process. I was assigned, along with several other officers, to conduct random searches of cells. Technically, an inmate was permitted to possess only the items issued to him by prison authorities. Everything else was considered contraband, although some leeway was extended. A cell shakedown was a search of every square inch of a cell and its contents, carried out in such a manner that the cell was left exactly as it was before the search, except for the presence of any contraband that might have been confiscated. Most of the inmates were at work or in the yard during the search, but occasionally we came to an occupied cell. Many of the prisoners resented being disturbed in this way, while others cooperatively submitted to the search.

During the ensuing three or four weeks, I made the rounds of all the duty stations I would be expected to man on the island. I worked in all the armed posts such as the towers, yard wall, and gun galleries. These armed posts were sited at strategic places about the prison, and the weaponry varied according to the specific purpose of the station. The Alcatraz guns included the 12-gauge riot shot gun, a .45 caliber automatic pistol, a .30 caliber bolt-action rifle, and the .45 caliber Thompson submachine gun made so famous as the "tommy gun" used by both gangsters and law enforcement officers during the roaring Prohibition days. A weapon new to me was the 1.5 caliber gas gun, which could fire both long- and short-range tear gas projectiles. It was an effective weapon, but during my entire employment at Alcatraz, I never saw one used against an inmate. I also visited all the work areas, including the prison laundry, tailor shop, blacksmith shop, carpenter shop, and shoe repair plant. My tour of instructional visits took me to the kitchen, the bakery, the hospital, and the clothing room, where prisoner clothing and linen were stored and issued.

The Alcatraz kitchen was a state-of-the-art food processing facility with the most modern cooking equipment. Food was prepared by inmate culinary workers under the supervision of a chief steward and his staff. The position of steward in any prison is a job requiring considerable ability. He must serve nutritious and tasty food, yet be ever watchful for waste. Inmates had no compunction about surreptitiously destroying or wasting food. Food riots brought about by unpalatable prison meals were problems in some penal institutions. That was never the case at Alcatraz, where the food was excellent and plentiful.

Food was served cafeteria-style in the mess hall from steam tables. The inmates filed into the mess hall according to cell numbers and received their food on steel trays. They could have as much as they wanted, but had to eat all that they took. From the steam table they proceeded to prearranged seating at tables of ten. Seconds were available on a rotating schedule, starting with a different table at regular intervals. While the food was institutional in style and presentation, it was tasty and nutritious, the same as that served in the officers' mess. Not surprisingly, though, the inmate cuisine could not compete with Eunice's cooking.

The United States Department of Public Health supervised the Alcatraz hospital, which was managed by a chief medical officer, with an assistant and a dental officer. All three were commissioned officers in the United States Public Health Service. In addition, several inmate "guard attendants" (paramedics) assisted in the maintenance of the prisoners' health. All the inmate medical workers as well as the patients were under the supervision of custodial officers assigned to the hospital.

A major feature of our indoctrination was physical conditioning and training. We received instruction in judo and boxing as well as a vigorous calisthenics course. Self-defense and hand-to-hand combat training were emphasized throughout the training period. Handball and other conditioning drills were part of the program, and although several of the new men suffered minor injuries, most of us survived the program in noble fashion.

In the evening after the inmates were locked in their cells, we received firearms instruction, and often the night quiet would be shattered by the sounds of rifles and pistols on the firing range. Since the gunfire was audible to the inmates who celled on the east side of the cellhouse, I often wondered what went through their minds as they listened to us blaze away on the range. Was it a warning against attempting escape, or was it a further challenge to beat the system? Physical training and weapons training were in addition to our regular custodial duties. Since most of the trainees were assigned to one of the night shifts, it made for long workdays and a paucity of sleep. Recreational activities were not part of the program, and our limited free time was mostly spent just resting.

Finally, there were a couple days of testing covering policy, procedure, operations, physical performance, and weapons expertise. With the six-week training period at an end, we were assigned to one of a number of posts in the regular prison routine. We proudly took our place as part of the custodial force at one of the most famous prisons in the world.

Ernest Lageson, junior custodial officer.

Chapter III

Alcatraz, the Prison

The mystique that surrounded the island prison carried with it an aura of the ultimate in human incarceration that meant different things to different people. To many it meant dark, damp "Spanish" dungeons hewn out of solid rock in San Francisco Bay. To most inmates in the federal prison system, it meant the end of the road, while to others, it meant the beginning of the road back. But to most people, Alcatraz was where the federal prison system kept its most dangerous and escape-prone convicts.

Although the federal system is considered the leader in penal organization and inmate treatment, it is one of the youngest systems in the country. While the army and navy have operated military prisons since revolutionary days, it was not until 1891 that the federal Bureau of Prisons, as it is known today, came into existence. Prior to that, federal prisoners were housed in state prisons with the cost being borne by the federal government. When this became too costly, three federal prisons were opened. The first of these was Fort Leavenworth, Kansas, an army prison, which was turned over to the Department of Justice to become a federal penitentiary. A federal prison was constructed in Atlanta in 1902, and a territorial jail on McNeil Island in Puget Sound, Washington, was converted into a federal penitentiary.

During the years that followed, the system grew and matured until there were federal institutions to house all types of offenders. Prison camps housed minimum custody inmates; correctional institutions held those convicted of more serious offenses; and penitentiaries contained the most dangerous prisoners.

Reformatories housed young offenders. Women inmates were confined in a separate facility. Finally, a state-of-the-art medical and psychiatric facility was constructed at Springfield, Missouri.

The penitentiary population ranges from the improvable, rehabilitative types to the intractable and habitual. The most troublesome of this latter group were confined on Alcatraz. On January 1, 1934, Alcatraz was officially designated a federal penitentiary, and in August of that year the first inmates arrived. Prisoners considered incorrigible in Leavenworth, Atlanta, and McNeil Island were sent via specially designed prison rail cars to the island prison. A few inmates from other institutions were also transferred here, and the Alcatraz mystique was born. Over the years approximately 1570 men served time on Alcatraz. The average number of prisoners at any one time was 270 to 280.

Alcatraz Island and San Francisco Bay were first viewed by Europeans in 1769, when a Spanish overland expedition from a settlement in San Diego in search of Monterey Bay missed its goal and discovered San Francisco Bay. It was not until 1775, however, that the bay and its islands were explored and mapped. On August 5 of that year, Don Juan de Ayala sailed into the bay aboard the Spanish packet boat *San Carlos*. Inside the harbor, he encountered a small island that presented a stunning sight. It appeared to be of white rock, with thousands of roosting birds. The island was actually limestone covered with hundreds of years of bird guano. One story has it that, impressed by the number of pelicans he saw on the small outcropping of rock, he named the island *Isla de los Alcatraces*, Spanish for "the Island of the Pelicans."

For nearly a century after its naming, the island remained the province of the local sea birds. When California became a state in 1850, Alcatraz became federal property, and the first military command was established there in 1859. Cannon, wharves, and a lighthouse were installed, and the island was soon fortified. In 1868, the army designated Alcatraz as a disciplinary barracks for its long-term military prisoners. As an army prison, Alcatraz held many famous Indian leaders, captured during the Indian wars. Also incarcerated were military prisoners of the Philippine Insurrection, Spanish-American War, Boxer Rebellion, and World War I. During the earthquake and fire of 1906, prisoners from the San Francisco county jail were temporarily housed on the island.

In 1934, the Bureau of Prisons took over the island and converted it into a bastille to hold incorrigible federal prisoners. All efforts were advanced to make the new maximum-security prison as impregnable as possible: tool-proof cell bars, new guard towers, floodlights, metal detectors, and tear gas dispensers. When the new institution was ready for occupancy, experienced officers from several of the older federal prisons were transferred to The Rock. Inmates from the other institutions were screened and the most notorious discipline problems and escape-risks were transferred to the new escape-proof facility.

Red buoys anchored 200 yards off the island were silent sentinels, warning all watercraft to stay beyond the confines of the markers. In the early days of the prison's operation, curious sightseers frequently couldn't resist the temptation of taking a close look at The Rock, and would steer their boats inside the buoys. These trespassers were often greeted by a shot across the bow from one of the strategically located guard towers. This so frightened and angered some that they complained to the local civil authorities and the Coast Guard. Although the officers were not in violation of any law, such aggressive warning measures were frowned upon by the prison administration, and were soon curtailed.

While armed tower guards and barbed wire impediments at key points served to dissuade escape attempts, the principal constraints against such ventures were the cold water and strong tides surrounding the island. Another obstacle to inmate freedom was the sheer rocky cliffs. Lest these manifestations of confinement were insufficient to the outside observers, a huge sign on the island beach facing San Francisco admonished all viewers:

WARNING
PERSONS PROCURING OR
CONCEALING ESCAPE OF
PRISONERS ARE SUBJECT
TO PROSECUTION AND
IMPRISONMENT

The entrance to the island was the large concrete dock on its east side over which another mammoth sign proclaimed to all passing boat traffic:

UNITED STATES PENITENTIARY
ALCATRAZ ISLAND AREA 12 ACRES
1 1/2 MILES TO TRANSPORT DOCK
ONLY GOVERNMENT BOATS PERMITTED
OTHERS MUST KEEP OFF 200 YARDS
NO ONE ALLOWED ASHORE
WITHOUT A PASS

The dock was an incredibly busy venue. Through here passed not only all residents and visitors to the island, but all food and supplies. Everything and everybody arriving on the island was searched by hand, electromagnetic metal detector, or both before leaving the dock area. While metal detector searches are part of life today, they were virtually unknown in 1940s. Then, they were state-of-the-art security devices used in only the rarest of instances. Most members of the public were not even aware of their existence.

The metal detectors at locations on the island traversed by the prisoners were fine-tuned to detect even the smallest pieces of metal, whereas the one on the dock was set to detect large metal masses such as guns and knives. Sensitive situations periodically developed when the metal stays in the undergarments of female visitors would set off the machine. Since there were no female employees at Alcatraz, the dock officer was required to exercise considerable discretion and diplomacy in clearing the visitor, particularly if it was an inmate's visitor entering the cellhouse. In addition to visitors, sacks of bulk food products such as sugar, flour, rice, and similar commodities were routinely passed through the "snitch box," as the metal detectors came to be known, before being taken to the kitchen and other areas of the prison where they would come in contact with inmate workers.

The cellhouse was located at the highest point of the island, and was virtually a city under one roof. In addition to the individual cells, the huge building housed the kitchen, bakery, dining hall, shower room, clothing and linen dispensary, hospital, activity rooms, library, chapel/movie theater, as well as the storage and utility facilities necessary for the operation of the prison. In addition to the general population cell blocks of B and C, there was D Block, the isolation section of the prison. Here, as noted earlier, were confined the incorrigibles of the incorrigibles. If, for whatever reason, an inmate could not get along in the general population of Alcatraz and had to be segregated, he went to D Block.

Alcatraz was designed to hold the worst of the habitual, intractable prisoners of the federal government, and the inmates incarcerated there did not come directly from court. Every federal prisoner was given the chance to demonstrate his ability to be rehabilitated while serving his sentence. Consequently, federal felons were initially placed in one of the less-restrictive institutions. There they were given the opportunity to straighten out their lives. Those who rejected this alternative and became troublesome inmates in a medium-security facility were sent to Alcatraz. The island prison became the maximum-security institution in the federal prison system. As noted previously, for some men, it was the end of the line. For others, however, it proved to be the first step on the long road back to freedom and respectability.

Prison dining hall during mealtime. The steam table is visible in the background.

Shoe shop

Tailor shop

Machine shop

Cargo net shop

Laundry

Furniture shop

Bakery

Inmates repaired and repainted the buoys used to hold the anti-submarine net in place across the Golden Gate.

West gun gallery

Road tower and catwalk to top of wall around recreation yard. Prison industry buildings in background.

"Broadway" looking north toward dining room.

Chapter IV

Island Home

About half of the approximately one hundred employees and their families lived on the island. While senior officials such as the warden, associate warden, and captain of the guard were required to live on the island, for most employees, it was a matter of choice.

The living accommodations were primarily apartments. The largest of these, Building 64, was a former barracks building just above the dock that had been remodeled into a twenty-seven-unit apartment house. The apartments ranged in size from one to four bedrooms, and the rooms were large and comfortable. The modest rent ($25/month for a two-bedroom unit) included a fully furnished apartment and all utilities. So, in addition to a significant salary increase, we were spared the expense of replacing all our furniture that Eunice had sold at auction before she and young Ernie left North Dakota to join me on The Rock. Just prior to World War II, the bureau constructed another apartment building on the southwest side of the island, known prosaically to island residents as the New Apartment Building. Of Art Deco design, it contained eighteen beautifully furnished, spacious apartments. It was occupied by the more senior employees and commanded higher rents than Building 64. Housing was determined on a seniority basis, and we were not on the island long enough to qualify for residence in the New Apartment Building. There was always a waiting list for island housing. There were also four single-family cottages, a new building for the bachelor officers near the New Apartment Building on the parade ground, and another bachelor officers' quarters building on the dock. The BOQ building on the dock was originally the site of the livery stable during army days.

The three most opulent residential structures on the island had all been constructed by the army. The warden's house, elegant with its fourteen rooms, multiple fireplaces, and dramatic wood paneling, was constructed by army convict labor in 1922. It was of California Mission style, with breathtaking views of the bay, the bridges, San Francisco, and the surrounding communities. Dr. Romney Ritchy, the prison physician, lived next door to the warden in an equally large but less ostentatious home. Victorian in design, the doctor's home also dated from army days. On the parade ground at the far southeast end of the island was a spacious and stately duplex occupied by the associate warden and the captain.

Social life on the prison islet was limited by both circumstances and geography. It was small town life in the heart of a major metropolitan area. The handball court in the small gymnasium on the parade ground was a source of enjoyment for the more active men. Much recreation time was spent in the bowling alley, located in the basement of the large social hall near the dock. There were organized bowling leagues, with tournaments and cash prizes. Pocket billiards and pool tables were also available in the recreation room. The main floor of the hall was the site of most of the organized family social activity. The large hall had both a stage and a kitchen, and enough room to serve over a hundred people at a sit-down meal.

During holidays, the Officers' Club usually hosted a dinner for all the folks on the island. Christmas was always a major event, with a big party for the children and a visit from Santa Claus. In those years, Santa bore a striking resemblance to Ed Schneider, the jovial and somewhat overweight Coast Guard chief petty officer who operated and maintained the lighthouse. Halloween was another huge party for the kids. They all paraded around the hall showing off their costumes, then took part in an evening of games, dining, and fun.

Fishing was a popular recreational activity for the Isaac Walton types. Unlimited fishing was permitted from the dock after 4:30 p.m., when the prisoners returned to the cellhouse. Fishing from the island's beaches was permitted anytime. Since Alcatraz was a federal reservation, no license was needed and there was no fishing season with which to be concerned. In addition, fishing at night from the dock using floodlights was permissible. When the fish were running, large catches were common, particularly of sea bass. One such catch was so massive that fish were presented to all the island residents, served in the prison dining room, and given to all the boat crews that made calls to the island. Some island fishermen became so expert that they would fish from specific locations on the island depending upon what species of fish they were seeking.

The activities for the women were typical of the times. The Red Cross had organized a group on the island to prepare bundles to send to the troops overseas. Many of the wives worked outside the home, and commuted daily to jobs in the city. The early forties saw, for the first time, women moving in large numbers from the home into the workforce, and Alcatraz enthusiastically joined that national trend. The ladies also organized their numbers into various bridge, canasta, book, and sewing clubs, as well as other interest groups typical of small community life. Many women took an active interest in the island bowling activities, and there were ladies' leagues as well as mixed leagues. One of the best bowlers on the island was Billie Pepper, an officer's wife, who competed successfully in matches throughout Northern California.

Play activity for Alcatraz children was generally confined to the parade ground. This area, which had previously heard the beat of military boots, was a vast expanse of concrete covering the southeast end of the island. Now on the parade ground were heard the squeals of small children, the sound of roller skates, softballs being hit, and the general din of childhood play. It was the Alcatraz equivalent of a large, inner-city playground. A great deal of the time, the area was swept by gusty winds blowing in through the Golden Gate, which annoyed the adults but never seemed to bother the children. Several enterprising officers erected swings and other playground equipment in a huge sand enclosure, which greatly aided the mothers of small children. While there was plenty for the younger kids to do, teenagers found much less in which to be involved unless they were active hobbyists. Fortunately, society at the time was such that children were relatively safe in public, and the island children of all ages frequently made their way to San Francisco to attend movies, athletic contests, or just "hang out in town." I particularly recall young Ernie and his friends regularly attending Saturday movies by themselves in the city when they were only ten or eleven years old. The only admonition from his mother and I was that he be on the 5:10 p.m. boat from San Francisco to be sure he was home in time for dinner.

There were some activities totally indigenous to Alcatraz that the children regularly enjoyed. Riding the boat to school each morning and living on one of the most famous islands in the world made the "Alcatraz kids" mini-celebrities at the various San Francisco schools they attended. The island children could also host their friends from school, which only added to their popularity. The young boys on the island took the age-old game of cops and robbers to the indictment and conviction step and played prison. In that game, the make-believe characters were guards and cons, with the latter group constantly trying to break out of prison. There were also the periodic, beachcombing trips to out-of-the-way sections of the island's rocky coast in search of "neat stuff" that frequently washed ashore. Just sitting on the seawall observing the ship traffic entering and leaving the bay was a pleasant experience for the observer of any age. The bay, the ship traffic, and the view were never the same, always interesting and beautiful. The bay was teeming with warships, sleek destroyers, majestic cruisers, daunting aircraft carriers, troop transports en route to the South Pacific war zone, and merchant ships from all over the world.

There were a number of prohibitions that the young Alcatraz resident had to accept. Not surprisingly, toy weapons were not permitted on the island. Facsimile guns, knives, swords, clubs, even water pistols, were strictly forbidden. Since whistle signals were used to control inmate movements in the cell house, toy whistles were also prohibited. Because of space limitations, dogs, cats, and large pets were not permitted. Fish, turtles, hamsters, and anything that lived in a bowl or a cage were acceptable. While tricycles were allowed for the little ones, two-wheelers for the older crowd were forbidden. In later years, bicycles were permitted.

Because of the wartime gas shortage and limited parking near the dock, many of the island families, including ours, did not own automobiles. Despite this, most residents spent what time they could away from the monotony of the island. Probably the most aggravating inconvenience of life on Alcatraz was the constant fear of missing the boat back to the island. The boat schedule was chiseled in stone, and the vessel waited for no one, except the warden and his wife. We often joked about the large number of movie endings we had to forgo to be sure we caught a convenient boat home.

Adverse weather was another factor with which the island dwellers had to contend. Occasionally, during winter storms, the bay waters became too rough for small boat traffic, and the island launch did not run. That meant no school for the children, a day off from work for the wives employed in the city, and a reshuffling of work schedules to cover for the non-resident officers who couldn't get to work. In winter, wind-driven rain frequently pelted the island. One officer described the Alcatraz rain accurately when he observed: "When it rains on Alcatraz, it rains in every direction, including up." Once, we were isolated on the island for two days during a storm, and the launch was moored to a pier in San Francisco to protect it from the turbulent waters around the island. The freight and water boats didn't leave their mainland moorings, and no one came to or left the island. It was my misfortune to have my days off fall during that storm, and I had to cover for off-island officers who couldn't get to work. Fortunately, such violent weather was rare. One saving feature, however, was the absence of mud. While mud had been a major problem on the dirt and gravel roads of North Dakota, there was no such problem on Alcatraz, where nearly every outdoor surface was either rock or concrete. So while there was a lot of wet weather, it was a clean wet.

Unquestionably, the island's most dramatic climatic condition was the fog. During the summer months, the high temperatures in the Sacramento Valley a hundred miles east of San Francisco caused the hot air to rise. This massive displacement of inland air drew cool marine air from the Pacific through the Golden Gate, producing a thick blanket of fog over San Francisco Bay. As the heavy finger of fog streamed through the gate, the first point of land it engulfed was Alcatraz. In winter, heavy dark advection fog often hugged the bay, totally obscuring vision. At times when I occupied the main tower, on the roof of the cellhouse, I saw Sausalito, Oakland, San Francisco, and the surrounding Bay Area communities drenched in sunlight, while Alcatraz was shrouded in fog. It was customary during heavy fog to keep the inmates in their cells until there was some clearing before sending them down to the work area. Some days, there was no clearing and the prisoners left their cells only for meals. While foggy weather prompted fear within the administration of escape attempts, and some did occur, trying to escape in the fog was virtually suicidal. Once away from the island in the fog, an inmate would be totally disoriented and unable to see landmarks to assist him in reaching the mainland. Every escape attempt in the fog was doomed from the start, and they all failed. But then, all escape attempts from Alcatraz failed.

On foggy days, one was keenly aware of the monotonous, booming sound of the foghorns, but soon learned to ignore it. The foghorns affected sleep patterns in various ways. If you went to sleep during clear weather, you would probably be awakened if they began to sound in the middle of the night. If you went to sleep listening to them, you would probably be awakened in the middle of the night if the weather cleared and the foghorns stopped sounding. And there were some poor souls who had trouble sleeping at all if the horns were sounding.

While a complicating factor of island sleep, fog was a major hazard to navigation. When acting as the boat officer in heavy fog, I would station myself at the forward most point on the bow and peer into the blinding fog to guide the boat to our San Francisco pier. I developed an intimate knowledge of the fog sounds of the bay, including the various bell buoys, foghorns, and other identifying sounds and signals both on the bay and along the shore. Heavy fog at night was our worst navigational nightmare.

Alcatraz regulations prohibited alcoholic beverages on the island. This, of course, was impossible to enforce, and clandestine drinking was the rule rather than the exception. Cautious imbibing was generally practiced because there was always the possibility of an emergency requiring the sober attention of all off-duty officers living on the island. An officer on Alcatraz was never totally off-duty.

A humorous sidelight to island partying was the disposal of "empties." Obviously, the spent Scotch, bourbon, or gin bottles could not be discarded in the island garbage cans, as such an open violation of regulations would require the officer supervising the garbage crew to report the infraction, thereby prompting an investigation. Hence, it became necessary to find another method of disposal. Living on an island made the task relatively simple, albeit a bit inconvenient. One would slip quietly to the far end of the island in the dark of night with a bag of bottles empty of liquor, but full of water, and with a mighty heave, hurl them into the swirling currents to sink silently to the bottom of the bay, perhaps to become a part of some future archeological study.

New Year's Eve was celebrated in various ways. Of course, some of us were on duty. Those who were not generally planned parties at home or in the city. I recall one New Year's Eve when Eunice and I, along with several island friends, spent the evening prowling San Francisco's famed International Settlement. This was the former site of the notorious Barbary Coast of old San Francisco, which in the 1940s was the center of the city's nightlife. We concluded the evening with a large group of island folk at Izzy Gomez's, the well-known refreshment emporium on Pacific Avenue. It was a happy, noisy assembly that boarded the 12:30 a.m. boat that New Year's morning, and during the ride back home, a lively discussion ensued centered on whether or not, considering our condition, we were bringing alcoholic beverages onto the island in violation of island non-alcohol regulations. The dock officer saw fit to overlook the potential violations, and, after wishing all of us a Happy New Year, waved us off to deal with morning headaches.

But not all island partying was dealt with benignly. On occasion, an officer would have imbibed a bit too freely, which was evident upon his return to the island. This was considered a breach of conduct, which could result in an appearance before the warden and a letter of reprimand going into the individual's personnel file. While prison guards, like everyone else, exhibit human frailties, where those involved alcohol, there was little tolerance on Alcatraz. It was further evidence that Alcatraz was a special place, and the men who worked there had special responsibilities.

Religious life on the island was left up to the individual families. While Catholic, Jewish, and Protestant services were available for the inmates, no services of any kind were provided for the employees or their families. A Protestant Sunday School class was organized at one point and met with both success and failure, depending upon the quality of the adult teachers. Given the logistics involved, the number of worshipers who made the Sabbath trek to San Francisco was limited.

Like the rest of the nation, Alcatraz was profoundly affected by World War II. Soon after the December 8, 1941, declaration of war, major changes came to the island. Two anti-aircraft guns were mounted at opposite ends of the cellhouse roof.

Another was installed on the roof of the Model Shop Building at the northwest end of the island, and a fourth on the roof of the New Apartment Building. About fifteen soldiers were stationed on the island to man the weapons. The gun crews were billeted in the solarium, a large open area occupying the top floor of the New Apartment Building. In time, the soldiers became part of the island community and were particularly well received by the teenage girls. They were part of the Fort Mason Command in San Francisco, from which their meals were delivered three times a day in large thermal boxes. The solarium also contained cooking facilities, which permitted the soldiers a modest amount of culinary creativity.

The solarium encampment held a particular fascination for our young son. As the island newsboy, Ernie Jr. delivered papers to the island residents, including the soldiers. They befriended Ernie, including him in their meals and off-duty activities. Many of the soldiers were teenagers who treated Ernie as a younger brother, all to his delight. With the departure of the guns and soldiers following World War II, the solarium became the site of island social events, replacing the aging social hall.

Medical care for island residents left much to be desired. While the Public Health Service provided full medical and dental care for the prisoners, no such care was available to the civilian population. Alcatraz residents received only emergency medical care on the island, unlike the military dependents on nearby Angel Island, who received full medical and dental care. Medical benefits were not part of the Bureau of Prisons employment package, and medical insurance as it is known today was not generally available. Medically, you were on your own. The most the Alcatraz folks received in this regard was a special boat trip to the mainland if the medical emergency appeared sufficiently serious. Men injured in the line of duty were eligible to receive treatment at the Marine Hospital in San Francisco. All civilian medical care had to be arranged individually on the mainland, which was difficult.

The basic employment benefits of today were not available to employees of the Bureau of Prisons in those days. One of the most egregious incidents of deficiency followed the death of Officer Bill Miller during the 1946 escape attempt. Bill, like me, was taken hostage, and he was killed. His wife and children received virtually nothing by way of pension or burial expense, and a collection was taken on the island to send Bill's body to Pennsylvania for burial. The family received pension benefits of only about fifteen dollars per month, and suffered enormous economic hardship for years after Bill's death.

The educational life of the island children began each morning with a boat ride to school, and at the end of the day, another boat ride home. During the war years, the small army passenger ship, the USS *General Frank M. Coxe*, supplemented the Alcatraz boat schedule with periodic stops at Alcatraz as it carried army passengers between Angel Island and San Francisco. Since Alcatraz was situated between Angel Island and the city, and both boats used the same dock on the mainland, it was only a minor imposition on the army. One of these daily stops made by the *Coxe* was at 8:20 a.m. to pick up the school children. It was always a source of envy by the Alcatraz parents that government busses met the army children and delivered them to their schools, while our children had to walk. This was due, no doubt, to the more expansive employee benefits provided by the War Department as compared to the Department of Justice, which operated on a tighter budget.

During the years we lived on the island, the entire Bay Area was subject to a partial blackout as a precaution against Japanese air attack. Because of our exposed position in the middle of the bay, those of us living on Alcatraz felt particularly vulnerable to such attack. There were several alerts, all of which were followed relatively soon by an "all clear" signal. One of these late-night alerts was designated a "red alert" and went on for much of the night. The entire Bay Area was totally blacked out, with only the moon and stars providing illumination. Officers went to every apartment, waking all the residents and alerting them to prepare to enter the air raid shelters. The offending aircraft proved to be a US Navy PBY flying boat returning from Pearl Harbor. Somewhere over the Pacific, the plane's radio went dead, and the pilot was unable to identify himself to coastline radar stations. Squadrons of fighter aircraft were dispatched to intercept the unidentified aircraft, and visions of another Pearl Harbor–type attack swirled about the Bay Area. Once the identification was made, the all-clear was sounded, and we all thankfully went back to bed.

A complete air raid shelter was established in the basement of Building 64 for the island residents. In case of attack, the inmates would have been moved to a shelter in the basement of the cellhouse. This was the site of the legendary "dungeon" cells, which served as solitary confinement in the early years of the prison. Not surprisingly, this air-raid plan differed significantly from the cellhouse rumor of the time. The story that circulated among the convicts was that in the event of a Japanese air attack, the guards would kill all the prisoners in their cells to prevent them from escaping.

During the very infrequent prison break attempts, there was understandable concern among the women and children of the island, since they all had husbands and fathers who would be involved should serious difficulties arise. The standing order on the island was that in the event of an escape attempt, the civilian population was to return to their apartments and lock their doors. When the escape siren sounded, that is exactly what happened.

An event that was always of interest to the island residents was the arrival of new prisoners. Inmate transfers always arrived on a special boat run. Prisoners and island residents never shared the same boat, so whenever the boat left the island at other than a regularly scheduled time, it meant something special, usually a prisoner shipment.

When the boat returned from a special run, the balconies of Building 64 were lined with curious observers. The officers were interested to see how many new inmates were arriving, and if any returnees were among them. The rest of the residents were merely curious. Such shipments were known as "chains," since the inmates arrived in handcuffs and leg irons chained together in a single line. Upon arrival, they were loaded on a truck for the trip "up top" to be "dressed in" as official Alcatraz prisoners. "Up top" was the descriptive term for the highest level on the island, the cellhouse, the lighthouse, and the homes of the warden, doctor, and lighthouse keeper.

The "new fish" (first-time Alcatraz inmates) were always quiet and apprehensive. At the north entrance to the cellhouse, the new prisoners stepped down from the truck and stood silently in single file. One by one, they were taken into the cellhouse where their shackles and civilian clothes were removed and they began the lengthy indoctrination process. Whoever they were, or thought they were, in their prior institution, at Alcatraz, each was just another number. His prison career was starting all over, and he was on the bottom rung of a very austere social ladder. Back down on the balconies of Building 64, the show was over, and the curious Alcatraz observers returned to their normal activities.

While Alcatraz, like most prisons, operated in a paramilitary style, during the off-duty hours there was only minimal class distinction among the island personnel. The lieutenants and other supervisory officers took an active part in most social activities. The warden was not an active participant in our general activities, but he and Mrs. Johnston often attended social gatherings as guests of the officers. Egalitarianism generally prevailed among the island employees. In addition to the various organized activities for the residents, there was the normal array of family activities common to small-town life. There were the few instances where some of the supervisors had difficulty associating with the "ordinary folks," and some of the wives tended to remain aloof from the "commoners," but these were isolated situa-

Building 64, the largest apartment house on the island. Originally a barracks during the army occupation, it was remodeled by the Bureau of Prisons into twenty-seven separate units for custodial officers and their families.

tions. Alcatraz was basically a friendly and cooperative community.

Fire protection on Alcatraz was excellent. Hydrants were placed at strategic points around the island and small shacks containing hose and hose carts were located nearby. The hydrants were pressurized from the island power plant and utilized water from the bay. The fire-fighting equipment included a fully equipped fire truck, kept in a constant state of readiness and regularly tested and inspected. Once each month, the officers were called out for fire drill, the hoses and engine were connected to the hydrants, and the pressures checked. The fire warning signal (drill or the real thing) was given from the powerhouse and sounded at various locations around the island. Many of those off the island, including the Coast Guard personnel, could also hear the signal. On more than one occasion, with the powerhouse whistle blaring its warning and we volunteer firemen and our fire truck spraying bay water from hoses on the dock, a Coast Guard cutter would cruise by just to be sure it was only a drill.

Telephone communication between the island and the outside world was available only from the administration office. There was only one official telephone line and it was controlled from the armory. There were two or three extension lines in the offices through the armory line. These phones were for official business only and were not available to the civilian population. Outside phone service for the island residents was a single pay phone in the administration office. Later, two more pay phones were installed, one in Building 64 and one in the New Apartment Building. Island residents were limited exclusively to a pay phone for outside calls. No island residence, including the warden's house, had a phone line off the island.

An intra-island telephone system was the only method of internal communication other than personal contact. All duty stations, work areas, offices, and residential areas could be reached by island phone. While most residences had an intra-island phone, this was not the case in Building 64. The twenty-seven apartments in Building 64 were served by six wall phones mounted as conveniently as possible. Each phone served from three to nine apartments, depending on the location. The system was similar to a boarding house arrangement where the residents shared a common telephone located in a hallway area. To reach a party, you dialed the phone nearest to their apartment, then asked whoever answered to notify your party.

Because of the high degree of cooperation among the residents, the system worked reasonably well. The arrangement did, however, place an added burden on the folks who lived near the phones. In many cases, it was just about as easy to go directly to the apartment you were calling to hold your conversation, particularly if one sought any degree of privacy, since all phone conversations took place in the hallways.

The time that our family resided on the island was among the happiest of our lives, in part because we were in California starting a new life. The excitement of the move, new surroundings, and the fascination associated with Alcatraz were all thrilling and exhilarating. Ernie Jr. was excited with life on the island, particularly his job as the island newspaper boy. At that time, San Francisco had four daily newspapers: the *Examiner* and *Chronicle* in the morning, and the *News* and *Call-Bulletin* in the afternoon. Ernie delivered all four papers, and turned a handsome profit for a lad of eleven. He met the first boat of the day on its return from San Francisco, with the morning papers. He would race around the island delivering his papers, then catch the 8:20 a.m. boat to school. He returned from school on the 3:45 p.m. boat, and his afternoon papers were on the ride back with him. His first act upon arriving on the island was to deliver the *News* and *Call-Bulletin*.

Eunice worked at several jobs in the city while we lived on Alcatraz. For a time, she worked in the Greyhound Bus Company offices. Later she was employed at the Federal Reserve Bank, and finally had a long-term position with the Alcohol Tax Unit of the Bureau of Internal Revenue. Her department supervised the federal taxation of the California wine industry, a position she thoroughly enjoyed.

In 1943, I enlisted in the navy to lend my humble assistance to what loomed as the mother of all battles, the Allied invasion of the Japanese homeland. Just before I entered the navy, we obtained an apartment at 1875 Sacramento Street in San Francisco, and the family remained there during my navy service. Upon my return in February 1946, I picked up where I had left off at the prison, but we remained in the city, and I commuted. I had decided to return to the life of education, but it was the middle of the academic year, and no teaching jobs were available. As a veteran, I was entitled to my old job back, so I returned to Alcatraz, never dreaming of what lay ahead for me in just three months.

The New Apartment Building completed by the Bureau of Prisons in 1934.

Cottages located on the east side of the parade ground occupied by employees and their families.

Parade ground and gymnasium, with warden's house *(right)*, lighthouse and lighthouse keeper's home *(left in background, upper level)*.

The little parade ground, located to the rear of Building 64, was used as a children's play area.

The motor launch *McDowell* used to transport island residents, employees, and inmates to and from Alcatraz from 1934 to 1945.

Motor ship *General Frank M. Coxe*, an army passenger vessel that operated between Fort McDowell on Angel Island and Pier 4 in San Francisco and supplemented the Alcatraz boat schedule.

Pier 4, the San Francisco dock used by both the *General Frank M. Coxe and McDowell*. Angel Island, Alcatraz, and the *Coxe* are visible in background.

Family outing in Golden Gate Park, San Francisco, 1942.

Lageson family on Alcatraz, 1943.

Ernie Jr. as the Alcatraz newspaper boy, 1943.

Ernest and Eunice on Alcatraz.

The Ernies, Jr. and Sr., during World War II, 1944.

A normal childhood on Alcatraz.

Children of Alcatraz waving to passing boats.

Children of Alcatraz with dock tower in background.

Children of Alcatraz, dock tower in background.

Children of Alcatraz on the island motor launch on their way to school in San Francisco.

Teenage Christmas party.

Home occupied by the Alcatraz prison doctor.

Warden's home.

A fully equipped air raid shelter was maintained in the basement of Building 64 during the World War II years for use by the officers and their families. A shelter was maintained for the prisoners in the basement of the cellhouse.

View of Alcatraz. From left to right on parade ground *(lower level)* the bachelor officers' quarters, the New Apartment House, fog horn *(small structure)* and duplex occupied by captain and associate warden.

Bowling alley in basement of Social Hall for the use of Alcatraz officers and their families.

Alcatraz Canteen, island grocery store for civilian residents.

Chapter V

Rules and Privileges

The general regimen at Alcatraz was probably similar to that of any major prison, but because of the inmates incarcerated there, some of the regulations made Alcatraz unique. While Alcatraz was considered a tough place in the early 1940s, it had been even tougher when it first opened. Until 1937, the Rule of Silence prevailed, under which inmates were forbidden to talk when in their cells or while in line moving to and from work, meals, and other destinations. Talking was only permitted at meals, at work, and in the recreation yard. When it was claimed that the strict rules were contributing to insanity and suicide attempts among the prisoners, conditions were somewhat relaxed. The Rule of Silence was one of the first regulations to be changed.

But even after the elimination of the Rule of Silence, an Alcatraz inmate had only four basic rights: food, clothing, shelter, and medical care. Everything else was considered a privilege subject to revocation. Inmates entitled to maximum privileges spent an average of fifteen to sixteen hours a day in their five-foot by nine-foot cells. These prisoners worked in one of the prison industrial jobs or at some other assigned job. Work was considered a privilege, and was cherished by most inmates. Those who didn't have jobs were in their cells almost continuously except for meals. For those who qualified, there was a recreation period in the yard for two to three hours on Saturday and Sunday. Despite the strict rules and the limited privileges, Alcatraz had one benefit enjoyed by few other federal prisons. One man per cell was the rule at Alcatraz, and it provided the prisoners with a priceless degree of privacy not generally available elsewhere.

The cellhouse contained four cell blocks. A, B, and C Blocks were in the main cellhouse while D Block, the isolation section of the prison, was in a walled-off area separate from the main cellhouse. The cells in A Block had never been upgraded from army days, and still contained the flat, non-tool-proof bars in use before the turn of the century. These cells were used as storage areas only, and did not hold prisoners. B and C Blocks had been upgraded and were home to the Alcatraz general population. Each block contained sixty cells in each tier and they were three tiers high, for a total of 360 cells in those two blocks. D Block contained another forty-two cells. The total prisoner population never even approached the maximum number possible.

The assignment of inmates to the various cells was generally random, with two major exceptions, both based on segregation common to the social order of the time. Black prisoners celled together in one area of B Block, and homosexual inmates were grouped together. The one homosexual black prisoner presented the administration with a quandry, but during most of my time on the island, this man was in D Block, where no segregation existed. Alcatraz segregation was not a policy of discrimination, for all the prisoners were treated the same. They all worked together; played together in the yard; and attended movies, church, and other gatherings together. In D Block, the races also celled together. The vast majority of the black prisoners preferred the cell segregation, as did the whites. and most of the inmates of both groups were unconcerned about the matter.

The homosexual situation was different since there was considerable hostility directed toward homosexuals, both inside and outside of prison at that time. In the 1940s, homosexual conduct was a felony, and on Alcatraz, homosexuals were vilified and often beaten by heterosexual inmates. Segregation of homosexuals was principally a matter of safety and security. Since the prisoners were seated in the dining hall according to cell location, there was also segregation during meals. As noted, inmate segregation did not represent racial or sexual preference discrimination by the Alcatraz administration. Rather, it was how Alcatraz dealt with the social and legal standards of the time, and best protected the prisoners confined there.

Unlike most prisons, there was no inmate classification of "trusty." None of the inmates at Alcatraz were trusted, and no presumption in that regard was ever made. Most prisons had men who were accorded a degree of freedom during the workday, depending on the jobs to which they were assigned. This was absent at Alcatraz. Inmates were always under the direct control of officers or the surveillance of an armed guard in a tower. The closest thing to trusties were the passmen who worked in the warden's home. These men cooked for the warden and his wife and maintained their house, similar to domestic servants. Theirs was undoubtedly the best inmate job in the prison. Handpicked for the job, they were usually men who had flawless records at Alcatraz and were nearing discharge or transfer. It was common knowledge that Mrs. Johnston treated the passmen to very special perks. They were permitted to listen to the radio, read the daily newspaper, and, of course, eat virtually whatever they wanted from the warden's kitchen. Yet even these most reliable inmates had to make themselves visible to be counted every thirty minutes. They appeared on the side porch of the house, where they could be observed by the duty lieutenant in the cellhouse offices and added to the periodic prisoner count.

While some federal prisons had commissaries where the inmates could make small purchases with the money they earned, no such facility existed at Alcatraz. The inmates were provided with what they absolutely needed and little else. Those inmates who earned money for work done in the prison industries were permitted to spend it for various educational or enrichment items such as books, magazines, or specialized publications not available in the library. They could also purchase musical instruments and sheet music. Some men purchased paints, canvases, and other artist's supplies. Rather than spending their money, the inmates could save their earnings in interest-bearing accounts until discharge, or they could have their earnings sent to their families.

If he was a cigarette smoker, a prisoner drew unlimited bags of so-called "dust" tobacco and cigarette papers each week. The common brands of sack tobacco such as Bull Durham, Stud, and others were issued to any inmate requesting it. The inmates had to roll their own cigarettes, but there was no limit on how much they could have. At Christmas, each inmate was given a holiday package of candy and other sweets, as well as two packages of Camel, Lucky Strike, or another of the popular brands of tailor-made cigarettes. Pipe smokers were issued pipes at regular intervals or when needed. Pipe tobacco was provided in unlimited amounts.

Toilet articles were issued to each inmate upon his arrival and replaced as needed. Included in this packet was an aluminum drinking cup, an aluminum shaving mug, a shaving brush, double-edged razor, a small metal mirror, tooth powder, tooth brush, and toilet soap. Razor blades were distributed two times a week so an inmate could shave. The blades were picked up fifteen minutes after distribution and stored on a board maintained by the cell house officer, so each inmate always got his own blade. The blades were sharpened after each use by an inmate orderly under the close scrutiny of an officer, and new blades were issued every two weeks. Inmates with suicidal history were given locked razors requiring a special tool to open and remove the blade. This tool was maintained by the cellhouse officer.

Each cell was equipped with an immovable steel strap bunk fixed to the wall on one side and supported by steel legs on the other. There was a small folding table and seat also mounted on the wall. Each inmate was given two blankets, a mattress, and a pillow, and each week received two clean sheets, a pillowslip, and hand and bath towels.

The cleanliness of his cell was the responsibility of each prisoner, and cellhouse officers periodically inspected the cells. If a cell was not clean, the inmate was placed on report and called before the disciplinary board. He was initially warned, and if his housekeeping habits failed to improve, he was punished. The punishment would be loss of some or all of the inmate's few privileges.

The prison library contained more than 15,000 books. The library also subscribed to several magazines that were approved for the prisoners. These included acceptable publications such as *Time, Life, Colliers, The Saturday Evening Post, The American, Newsweek, Reader's Digest,* and *New Republic.* The pulp-type publications featuring crime stories and sensationalized writing were prohibited because of the subject matter and the fact that many of these publications permitted personal ads. There had been numerous instances in the past where jail breaks had been planned through such ads, and while it was a remote possibility in the case of Alcatraz, no chances were taken. This was the same reasoning that prevented the convicts from receiving daily newspapers. Some inmates subscribed to specialty publications not ordered by the library, such as art and technical publications. In some cases inmates would join together and subscribe to publications and share them.

An inmate library orderly was assigned to arrange for and deliver library materials to the inmates. Each prisoner was provided with a list of all the books and other reading material in the library and was free to order whatever he wished. The books, magazines, or other materials would be delivered to his cell and picked up when he was finished with them. In the case of subscriptions shared by more than one convict, the library orderly prepared a routing slip and circulated the publication. (In 1946, it was a library orderly who planned and led the most sensational escape attempt in the prison's history, the infamous Battle of Alcatraz.)

While newspapers were not permitted for security reasons, the inmates were not denied news. During World War II, there was great interest among the convicts in the progress of hostilities. To keep them abreast of war news, major news items were posted twice a day on a large chalkboard for all the inmates to read. Prisoner attitudes regarding the war varied. The majority favored an Allied victory, but there was a significant minority that hoped for an Axis conquest. These men believed they had been mistreated by society and felt they would receive better treatment from German and Japanese conquerors. One hardcore gangland hitman, who was a model prisoner and also a friend of mine, had a very professional approach to the war. "You know, Boss, if the Germans and Japs take over, they're gonna need guys like me to keep guys like you in line. Comin' out of stir, I'll be a top-notch candidate to be a government gun. How much better can that be?"

Prisoners were permitted to send out two personal letters per week. These letters went only to previously approved correspondents, and a log was maintained to enforce the rule. An inmate was permitted to receive two personal letters per week, also from approved sources. Other correspondence, such as communications from attorneys, the courts, or matters relating to any business affairs the inmate might have, fell into another category, and there was no limit on such mail.

All personal mail was painstakingly examined and censored. In fact, mail censoring was so important that an officer was assigned full-time to this activity. Incoming mail to inmates was opened, read, and examined for hidden writing or contraband. If the mail officer did not consider a letter proper for delivery to an inmate, it was sent to the captain or associate warden for evaluation. Letters were placed in new envelopes for delivery to the inmates, and the original envelopes were destroyed. All magazines and books delivered by mail to inmates had to have come directly from the publisher. Friends or family were not permitted to send books or magazines to the prisoners. There were certain correspondents to whom the inmates were permitted to write without fear of censorship. These individuals included the warden, the director of the Bureau of Prisons, and the attorney general. This was to encourage prisoners to express their wishes and desires to these officials, and also to provide a means of receiving information from informers. The prisoners were totally free to communicate with their attorneys without fear that any of the correspondence would be opened.

I spent several weeks handling inmate correspondence, and the variety of inmate mail was interesting. Several of the men wrote cheerful, newsy letters while others wrote dull, often bitter missives. Some displayed considerable intellect. The near-illiterates wrote letters containing only the barest of information concerning their health and their jobs. Immediately following the sensational escape attempt in 1946, a number of prisoners attempted to write vivid accounts of the gun battles, but these were returned with memos advising that only prison personnel would describe such matters. Cranks regularly wrote to inmates. Women wrote with propositions ranging from pen-pal status to marriage. Religious zealots showered the institution with soul-saving literature, sometimes directed to specific prisoners and at other times to the entire population, including the administration. While some of this unsolicited correspondence was clever or interesting, none of it ever reached the inmates. They saw nothing but approved, censored correspondence from approved correspondents.

The Alcatraz convict was allowed one visitor each month, a direct family member or someone approved by the warden, who personally approved all inmate visitors. There were no limits on visits by lawyers for the prisoners. The precise timing of a meeting with legal counsel was set by the warden's office, and a letter of authorization was sent to the attorney advising him of the time of the boat he was to take to the island. While the length of meetings with attorneys was open-ended, personal visits were usually limited to about two hours.

The visiting room at Alcatraz differed not only from the typical Hollywood version, but also from all such prison facilities at the time. The visitor was locked in a small room outside of the east wall of the cellhouse, and the inmate was in the cellhouse on the other side of the wall. The two viewed each other through an eight-by-four inch bulletproof glass window. Beneath the window were perforated steel plates through which the visitor and inmate spoke. An officer sat beside the visitor and another sat beside the inmate. It was necessary to speak loudly to be heard through the metal plate, so both officers could hear everything that was said by both parties. No physical contact between convict and visitor was possible. In later years, intercom telephones were installed, but everything else remained the same. Not many of the inmates received visitors because most of their families resided a considerable distance from the Bay Area. Those with relatives living nearby generally had their monthly visitors. If the prisoner was to be interviewed by an attorney or someone in an official capacity, such as law enforcement personnel, the meeting was held in the visitors' room. These meetings were given total privacy.

Inmates did not work on Saturday or Sunday, so if he was not on the restricted list, a prisoner could participate in a variety of recreational activities in the yard. There were team sports such as softball. Pickup games were often organized for a given day and leagues were formed whose play extended over several weeks. The games were played with as much intensity as any scholastic or collegiate contests. While tempers on the athletic field often flared, I don't recall any such dispute that escalated to violence. Perhaps this was because sports were a diversion from the daily grind of survival as an Alcatraz convict and not the situation the participants associated with the violence that was a part of prison life. Other prisoners spent their recreation period playing shuffleboard, pitching horseshoes, or playing handball. Handball courts were laid out on the concrete floor of the yard, and the wall served as the backboard. Several of the inmates became excellent handball players.

Some inmates simply walked around the yard in groups of two or three, talking quietly. I often speculated as to the topics of those hushed conversations: world politics, the war, plans for an escape, plots to kill another inmate, cellhouse gossip, memories of their days of freedom, all of these and perhaps many more? Other men simply sat alone on the steps of the yard bleachers and gazed over the wall at the Golden Gate, San Francisco, and the ever-changing picture of ships, yachts, and other craft on the bay. We can only imagine what thoughts ran through the minds of those caged men as they sat silently and stared at the free world they had once known and some would never know again.

Card games were popular with the inmates. Bridge and pinochle were played during every yard period. Dominoes was another favorite. While card games were played continuously, standard playing cards were never used. Because the coating on playing cards could be scraped off to create a flammable, explosive mixture, prisoners were not permitted to have cards. This vacuum was quickly filled when the fertile convict mind created wooden card sets. These sets ranged from simple wood blocks with colored spots to elaborate inlaid sets made of fine woods and meticulously hand tooled. These wooden cards were manufactured in the prison wood shop and assigned to inmates who kept them during their stay on The Rock. The "cards" were shuffled by placing them face down on the playing surface and mixing them. Hands were drawn and placed upright on small slotted boards. From there the game proceeded as would any card game. Bridge was by far the most popular card game, and many of the prisoners were excellent bridge players. Many subscribed to bridge periodicals such as *Bridge World*, and the books on bridge were some of the most read volumes in the library. The bridge players were a group unto themselves. Their devotion to the game was all-consuming, occupying most of their leisure time. The bridge players also tended to be among the penitentiary's model prisoners.

I recall an exchange one weekend afternoon when a couple of sets of partners scheduled a game to 200,000 points. Not being a bridge player, I don't know how long it would take to play a 200,000 point game, but I assumed it would go somewhat beyond that Sunday afternoon. But then, those fellows had plenty of time for bridge, regardless of how many points were involved.

Gambling was prohibited, but, of course, it went on continuously. Since no currency or commissary tickets were in circulation, gambling existed in its simplest forms, and the convicts would wager virtually anything. They would bet their next piece of pie, or their next steak. But the basic cellhouse currency was hand-rolled cigarettes. Some prisoners maintained a cache of hundreds of cigarettes in their cells. Most of the inmates smoked, but even the nonsmokers trafficked in cigarettes as a means of gambling, paying debts, buying favors, or buying the various items of contraband that floated about the prison.

During recreation periods, the prisoners were favored with recorded music. In the morning, the speaker was placed in the yard, and in the afternoon the speakers were in the cellhouse for those not in the yard. The selections ranged from hillbilly and western recordings to semi-classical and classical numbers. Pop tunes were the most popular, and Bing Crosby and Dinah Shore were the favorite male and female vocalists.

Music was a significant part of inmate recreation, and was encouraged by the administration. In addition to being exposed to recorded music, prisoners were permitted to purchase musical instruments with their earnings, and many did. The prison had a number of instruments such as drums, bass viola, brass, and woodwinds, which were made available to inmate musicians. Several of the inmates were accomplished musicians, and others learned to play. The result was an inmate orchestra, The Rock Islanders. Their music was viewed as something less than mediocre by most of the officers and convicts, but the musicians considered themselves quite good. They practiced enthusiastically, and on holidays, they performed for the entire inmate population. Their concerts were generally well-received, perhaps because The Rock Islanders were the only live band in town.

A number of the prisoners were artists and worked in various mediums: oils, watercolors, pen and pencil sketching, and charcoal drawing. Some only dabbled at art, but others displayed considerable ability, and could probably have made a living in some artistic endeavor had they not chosen a life of crime. I was frequently saddened by the sight of a talented artist producing excellent work in prison, when with proper training and upbringing, he could have been making an honest, productive living in a creative field. Several of the artists received photographs of their families, from which they painted excellent portraits, and they were permitted to send the completed work back to their families.

The educational facilities at Alcatraz were limited because most prisoners had no interest in traditional education. Inmates who desired intellectual enlightenment were encouraged to pursue a program leading to a high school education or even college courses. Some inmates took advantage of this privilege, but most did not. Men hardened by a life of crime and incarceration displayed very little interest in education, even though the effort was made.

Several of the prisoners were avid readers and well-informed on many topics. The library inventory included fiction, biography, travel, numerous technical disciplines, law, and many other subjects. It was interesting to hear some of their discussions, which at times sounded more like a college faculty lounge than the nation's major maximum-security penitentiary. A few of the prisoners became "cellhouse lawyers" who bought many of their own law books and made themselves available to handle appeals for their contemporaries. Since there was little else for the inmates to do between final lockdown at 5:30 p.m. and lights out at 9:30 p.m. but read, the average literate inmate might read a hundred books a year. In addition, nearly all the inmates reviewed the many magazines that were available, even if all some did was look at the pictures.

Motion pictures were a major part of the recreational program at Alcatraz, and most of the inmates enthusiastically attended the screenings. They were shown twice a month, and attended by all but the few "hard heads" who didn't enjoy any form of recreation. Because a large number of inmates were concentrated in a relatively small area during movies, numerous officers were stationed in the auditorium, always alert for trouble. Heavily armed guards occupied the overhead gun gallery looking down on the moviegoers and the route they took to and from the auditorium.

Shown in the prison all-purpose room, the film could not begin until the prisoner count was complete and correct. An incorrect count and delay in the commencement of the movie brought howls of anger, despite the fact that none of the prisoners were going anywhere except to the movie, then back to their cells.

The films were usually musical comedy and similar light entertainment. Psychological and dramatic movies received little appreciation from the inmate audience, and were rarely shown. Comedy and musicals temporarily transported these caged men to a happier world, away from their depressing prison life. The prison administration understood this well, and heartily acceded to the inmates' entertainment desires. Such cheerful movies boosted convict morale and reduced tension. Newsreel and news documentaries were also popular, as most of the men were hungry for news of the outside world. The two most hated newsmakers of the time were President Franklin D. Roosevelt and J. Edgar Hoover, director of the

Federal Bureau of Investigation. Both men had played major roles in the development of the FBI, the law enforcement agency that put most of the Alcatraz convicts behind bars, and their image on screen brought instant negative reaction and name calling from the audience.

A resident Protestant chaplain and a Roman Catholic priest from San Francisco ministered to the spiritual life of the Alcatraz convicts. The Jewish prisoners were permitted special dietary accommodations during their religious holidays, and those interested received visits from rabbis. Not unexpectedly, when special Jewish foods were served, as many gentiles as Jews helped themselves to it. Catholic and Protestant services were held on alternate Sundays in the same auditorium that was used for motion pictures. The Protestant services consisted of the singing of a couple of hymns, reading of scripture, and a short sermon by the pastor. Catholic mass was the same as mass anywhere, with prisoners serving as altar boys. For many years, George "Machine Gun" Kelly was an altar boy. Not surprising was the fact that some of the inmates attended both Christian services. There were always individuals who took advantage of any open door, and went through it just for something to do. For some time, the Protestant chaplain permitted an inmate string band to play during the services, and the congregation remained after the service to enjoy a string ensemble jam session. As with movies, religious services brought extra custodial officers to guard against trouble. An armed guard also looked down from the gun gallery upon the religious ministrations. The presence of this armed guard—cradling his rifle and listening to the words of the Prince of Peace—was always ironic to me.

The Rock Islanders, Alcatraz inmate orchestra.

Inmate recreation yard.

All-purpose room in cellhouse, arranged for church service. It was also used to show movies and for other forms of entertainment.

Visitors' side of the visiting room after telephones had been installed.

Inmate side of the visiting area. Inmates sat in the cellhouse in front of small partitions with an officer seated beside them, and talked through a glass panel with their visitors on the other side of the wall.

Chapter VII

The Alcatraz Prisoner

There was no typical Alcatraz convict. Like any other segment of society, there was diversity and individualism among the men at Alcatraz. But there were a number of similarities among the men who wound up on The Rock. Every prisoner at Alcatraz had been assessed as incorrigible in some other federal prison and for that reason, was sent to the island penitentiary. Most were serving lengthy sentences and had long criminal records dating back to their teenage years.

The average Alcatraz convict was arrogant and egotistical. A typical Alcatraz inmate acted like a big shot, or as it has been appropriately phrased, "a legend in his own mind." He extolled his own criminal accomplishments while minimizing with disdain the exploits of his fellow prisoners. The amusing irony was that few, if any, believed the braggarts, and no one but the braggart really cared.

The typical Alcatraz inmate was eager to tell anyone who would listen what a tough guy he was. Perhaps it was ego or just part of staying alive in the underworld and prison, but they all had stories of their violent past, including gang warfare, individual battles, jail breaks, and shoot-outs with the police. Some of the men on The Rock really did qualify as tough, but most of those men spoke very little of their violent past. One learned about them from their files and the stories told by others.

The tough-guy issue was well summarized for me one day by one of Alcatraz's truly tough guys. In response to a known braggart's boasting, Bernie Coy proclaimed to me in disgust, "Those bastards aren't tough. You know, Mr. Lageson, there aren't no really tough guys in these joints. The tough guys are all dead. They shot it out with the cops and weren't taken alive." Ironically, in May 1946, Bernie

Coy proved his point. As the chief plotter and mastermind behind the most sensational escape attempt in Alcatraz history, Coy, along with two others, shot it out with the officers and was killed.

As the months, then years, of boring confinement wore on, men in prison developed a culture of curiosity. Snooping became a way of life. The monotonous, dull grind of prison routine turned them into the thorough investigators they so hated on the outside. They became incredibly curious, grasping at any small item of news or rumor that might spark their day. Many of the cellhouse gossips became irritating pests with their constant quest for up-to-date news of the outside. News magazines provided old news. What they were after was current information. The rumors that made the rounds were many and varied. They ranged from war and political news to cellhouse gossip. When anti-aircraft guns were mounted atop buildings around the island, the word circulated that "the joint was going to be broken up." It would be unsafe to keep imprisoned men in a place that was a military target, so the prisoners would be transferred to other prisons and Alcatraz would be closed. These rumors became so pervasive that even some of the island residents believed them, and a few families actually obtained barrels and crates to pack for the move.

One of the more fascinating recurring rumors dealt with transfers of new inmates to the prison. Word of an upcoming chain of new fish was exciting news, for it meant that inmates would be transferred from Alcatraz to other less restrictive institutions. Speculation then turned to who would be the likely transferees. The amazing thing was that these rumored arrivals and departures proved incredibly accurate as to time and number of inmates involved. It was an ongoing joke among the officers that some of the best-informed men on the island were inmates.

The war provided an endless source of rumors. An inmate plumber, Joe Mrozik, was a meddlesome busybody and the biggest gossip in the jail. One morning while I was serving as officer in charge of the cellhouse, he approached me with his pestering line of questions concerning the war. To end his annoying stream of inquiries, I responded with something less than full candor. "Well, Joe, I heard a report on the early news this morning that Hitler has been killed. Some reports had it as a suicide and others said he was murdered by some of his own people." Joe was astonished, and immediately cited some absurd reason why he had to be in the kitchen, and sought my permission to go. I was only too happy to grant his request. He was back within minutes telling me he had a job in the basement and again I let him dash off to spread the wonderful bit of news that only he possessed.

I noticed that he took a circuitous route to the basement so that he passed by the barbershop, where a number of inmates were waiting to get haircuts. After receiving their haircuts, they all went to their assigned jobs, so the word spread quickly through all the shops. When the work crews returned for the noon meal, the place was buzzing with the sensational news. But, alas, there was no suggestion of Hitler's death on the news board, and by the end of the day, Joe had been seriously discredited as a news courier. The next time I saw him, Joe admitted in sheepish good humor, "Boss, le'me tell you, I ain't never gonna ask you for news no more." And he never did.

Petty theft and smuggling contraband into the cellhouse were ongoing difficulties. The prisoners were constantly attempting to bring in braided rag rugs for their cell floor, as well as all sorts of gadgets and trinkets made illegally in the shops. The theft of civilian underwear in the laundry and civilian white shirts by the kitchen workers was a constant problem. Any item of personal property left unguarded was a target for convict thievery. Because it was so pervasive, minor infractions were frequently not even investigated, simply overlooked. Contraband was brought into the prison by either members of the custodial force or by the non-custodial clerks and foremen. Periodically, large amounts of such illegal items were found. Most of the contraband was harmless—gum, candy, cigarettes, pipes, even money. The mere existence of such unauthorized items, however, demonstrated violation of the rules by one or more employee. It was foolish, potentially dangerous, and illegal, and I never understood how inmates could cajole officers or staff into committing contraband violations.

The average inmate was obedient to prison regulations most of the time, but he didn't like it. I often thought that if these men had obeyed the laws of society while on the outside as well as they did while in jail, they could have gotten along quite well. In prison, armed guards and the threat of going to the Hole provided incentive for obedience. On the outside, people were guided by their consciences and sense of decency, which, unfortunately, most of the Alcatraz inmates did not have.

Few of the inmates demonstrated obvious resentment of authority, but in the hearts of most of them there burned a consuming hatred of law enforcement officers, including prison guards. Clear testimony of this was the open glee at the embarrassment of an incorrect count; the mutterings, hisses, and boos that arose when force was used to subdue fighting inmates; or when recalcitrants were forcibly escorted into isolation or solitary confinement. On the rare occasions when the escape siren blared, the cheers and shouts of encouragement for the escapees became a roar and were mingled with cries of "I hope the poor bastard makes it!" or "We hope you dirty screws never find 'em!" Most of the convicts were pleasant enough during the regular routine of the prison day. But should an officer be in a prisoner's way during an escape attempt, any hint of friendship would be gone. Pleasantness also disappeared any time an inmate was in violation of regulations and placed on report by an officer.

Almost to a man, the convict population made constant protestations concerning their convictions. Time and again I was told in all sincerity: "You know, Boss, I've done a lotta things that I coulda' gone to jail for, but I'm tellin' ya, this sentence is strictly a bum rap." Every man in Alcatraz seemed to have been sentenced on a bum rap. Based on my experience at Alcatraz, it could be convincingly argued that, from the prisoner's point of view, the number of unjust convictions in the federal court system was staggering. In fact, nothing could be further from the truth. Most of the Alcatraz convicts were either overtly violent or potentially violent. The majority of them were serving sentences for crimes of violence such as homicide, assault, robbery, kidnapping, rape, and other cruel or callous felonies. Not surprisingly, therefore, malicious and violent measures were frequently employed to resolve personal disputes in prison.

A typical example occurred one morning at breakfast when one of the mess hall waiters incurred the wrath of one of the inmate diners. Tony claimed the right to a second breakfast roll because his table was first in line to receive seconds at that meal. He accused the waiter of removing the platter before he could get his seconds, then delivering it to another table where a friend of the waiter was sitting. It was a quiet dispute without commotion, so no officer was aware that the disgruntled diner threatened the waiter. When Tony informed a buddy of the difficulty, plans were made to "get" the waiter. The angered convict and his friend worked as cellhouse clean-up orderlies, and planned to get the waiter when he returned to his cell after completing his morning kitchen duties.

When the waiter returned to his cell, the two assailants-to-be were sweeping nearby. But the waiter had been warned, and he too returned to the cellhouse with a buddy. When the waiter and his friend encountered the cellhouse orderlies, the affair exploded in all its fury. Brooms, mop handles, and hand brushes were flying wildly, as were fists, feet, and bodies. Another officer and I raced to the scene, and by the time we arrived, the attackers were receiving a painful lesson in street fighting. The kitchen workers had both been members of a notorious New York gang, and were far more adept at street warfare than their thoroughly outclassed aggressors. The larger of the two New Yorkers had Tony on the floor with his heel on the prone inmate's throat, and was about to grind down with all his weight when we threw him to the floor. I am certain that had we not intervened, Tony's prison sentence, and his life, would have ended right then and there. In the meantime, the alarm had been called to the armory, and the captain, associate warden, and several other officers responded immediately. The fracas was soon under control, and disciplinary action followed at once. Each of the participants was hustled off to a solitary cell for a few days of cooling off and reflection. I spoke to the big New Yorker some days later, and his analysis of the affair was simple. "Mr. Lageson, it was a damned good thing that you officers were there, because I was gonna to kill that little Dago queer." And I believed him.

On a subsequent occasion, another member of that same New York gang was involved in a particularly bloody fight. Though the altercation was quickly broken up, both men suffered injury, and the loser required hospitalization. The comments of the winner a few days later exemplified the cruel vein that ran through most of those men. By then, tempers had cooled and the incident was history, but the inmate's candor was chilling. "Lucky for both of us, Boss, that you guys came along. I would for sure have killed him, because when I get mad enough to fight a man, I'm mad enough to kill him." I believed that guy too.

Much has been written, fact and fiction, about the so-called code of the underworld. Nowhere is that code more fervently practiced than in prison. Here one sees overwhelming evidence of the fraternal feeling that binds the criminals together and against legal authority. At no time did the prison inmates demonstrate their adherence to the code more positively than during inmate fights and attacks. Innumerable cases are on record showing the universal refusal of one inmate to testify against another, regardless of the facts, the forum, or the gravity of the situation. It could be an informal questioning, a disciplinary board hearing, or a trial under oath. It could be a minor scuffle between inmates or a multiple murder. The response was always the same: "Gee, Boss, I didn't see a thing, and I didn't hear anything either." Part of the code was loyalty to contemporaries and hatred of the law, but fear of reprisal also was a factor.

In the case of a murder committed in the prison barber shop, witnessed by a half-dozen inmates, only one prisoner would identify the assailant. He was so frightened after the trial that he was assigned work that kept him away from the rest of the convicts, and at the earliest opportunity, he was transferred to another institution. During the trial, he commented to the officer escorting him to court, "Hell, I never got anything out of it before, so why should I 'dummy up' now? Maybe if I talk I'll get something done for me." He surely regretted his decision, because, despite his testimony, the defendant was acquitted. I don't know how he fared after his transfer, but the story of his "traitorous" testimony would have followed him to the new institution. At best, he would be looked upon with disdain and suspicion as a stool pigeon or cop lover. At worst, he would be the victim of revenge for his disloyalty. In any case, he did not have much reason for optimism regarding his future.

The criminal code was not absolute, and had its loopholes. The concept of "honor among thieves" is a complete myth. A criminal would double-cross a partner in a flash if he thought he could get away with it, and it happened all the time. While criminals worked together against law enforcement, they would readily work against one another if it was in their best interests.

A major exception to the criminal rule of silence was the cadre of prison informers, or "stool pigeons." Every prison has them, and it's doubtful that prisons would run well if they didn't have them. These inmates sought to further their own cause at the expense of their fellows, hoping for small privileges, transfers, and reduction of their sentences. The pigeon, also derisively known as a "fink," "rat," "snitch," and a few unprintable labels, was generally shunned by his fellow prisoners. Nobody said anything in the presence of a known stoolie that he didn't want passed on the screws. The stoolie listened intently to conversations, was alert for suspicious actions, and was always ready to pass information along to authorities.

Neither the officers nor the administration respected the informers, yet the information they provided was often highly useful to the successful operation of the prison. The officers never trusted the reports of a stool pigeon, but all of them were carefully investigated. You never knew what important information might come from a stoolie. You also never knew if he was telling the truth. They were never open about the information they supplied, but would pass it along in secret, always with the understanding that they would not be revealed as the source.

Informers often required special care in order to protect them from injury, and even death. They usually served a useful purpose for only a limited time, until the main body of convicts became aware of their acts of treachery. Following the stamp of disapproval by the general population, stool pigeons were assigned jobs that would keep them isolated from those men who might do them harm, and they were occasionally assigned cells where the officers were able to keep a watch over them. In rare cases, these prisoners were placed in isolation for their own protection, sometimes at their own request.

One reason for the distrust officers held for these snitches was that they would turn on officers as well as their own kind. I had occasion to experience the venom of one of these quislings when I was first assigned to work in the cellhouse as a new officer. This "friend of the custodial force" felt he was entitled to have his cell light on all afternoon, contrary to established regulations. Believing that his informer status afforded him favored treatment, the inmate attempted to go over the head of this new officer to the associate warden. When I refused his request to turn the light on, he announced that the lighting regulation did not apply to him because of his cell location, and it was in my best interests to turn his light on.

"I'll write a letter to the man, and make it mighty damn hot for you."

"Go ahead, write your letter," I responded, ignoring his threat.

The letter arrived informing authorities of my "cruel and inhuman treatment," but was disregarded without even an acknowledgment. My order stood, the lights remained dimmed, and the prisoner thereafter treated me with total respect.

Though we tried, no one totally understood the mental makeup of these captive humans and the reason for their often-inhuman actions. When one entered the prison for a day's work, he entered an entirely different world. He left behind the behavioral norms of the outside world, and to a large extent, lowered himself to the level of the criminals whom he watched. This transformation became necessary to cope with the conspiracy and intrigue that were always there. It was the first step in learning how to live with the inmates and control them.

Chapter VII

One Day in Twenty-five Years

To someone unfamiliar with prison life, it is difficult to comprehend the degree of confinement an Alcatraz convict experienced. The vast majority of an inmate's day was spent in his 9 ft. x 5 ft. cell. The men in general population, who enjoyed the most freedom, spent approximately fifteen hours a day during the week and sixteen hours a day on weekends and holidays locked in their cell. For the unemployed or restricted inmate, weekday cell time was twenty-two hours, and it was virtually twenty-four hours for the men in D Block. Despite this extraordinarily close supervision, a functional life had to be established in which all concerned could co-exist. Dangerous convicts had to be controlled, but their lives had to be made as comfortable as possible. The administration sought to accomplish some rehabilitation, regardless of how remote that likelihood might have been.

After a thirteen-hour night in his cell, the convict's day began early. The wake-up bell rang jarringly at 6:45 a.m., and the inmates had thirty-five minutes to clean up their cells and accomplish their morning personal care. During the night, a cellhouse officer had counted the inmates every hour. These counts were phoned to the armory, where a master sheet was kept day and night. Periodic counts of the inmates went on continuously, twenty-four hours a day.

At 7:20 a.m., the bell sounded, directing the inmates to stand silently at their cell doors for the first morning count. When the count was complete and correct, the captain blew his whistle, and the prisoners stepped back from their cell doors. At 7:25, on whistle signal from the captain, the cell doors opened, and the inmates stepped into the open doorway, but remained in their cells. Two minutes later, again on whistle signal, the inmate body moved along the galleries, down the steps at the end of the gallery, and into the mess hall.

The inmates entered the dining room in two lines and proceeded to the steam table at the far end of the room near the kitchen, where they received their food on steel trays. They then went to their assigned tables, each of which was set for ten. The morning meal generally consisted of cereal, rolls, and toast. Coffee and water were in pitchers on each table. Mealtime was usually one of the most important times of the day for the prisoners. It was one of the few pleasures in the life of an Alcatraz convict. Should an inmate leave a large amount of food, he was placed on report for wasting food. The usual punishment for such a violation was deprivation of meals. This was a stiff penalty, for, as an inmate once told me: "Boss, if you lose just one meal in one of these joints, it takes you weeks to get caught up again."

At the end of the meal, there was another count before the diners were permitted to leave. This time it was a silverware count. Every implement on each table had to be accounted for before anyone left the room.

Trousers and shirts were worn at mealtime and coveralls were worn at work, so once back in their cells, those prisoners working outside the cellhouse immediately changed clothes. At 7:55 a.m., whistle signals directed the inmates, first to stand at their cell doors, then to proceed along the tiers to the cellhouse floor and into the recreation yard. Here they lined up according to job location and waited for their supervisors to escort them to their work sites. As they filed out of the cellhouse, they were counted once again.

There were a dozen or so work sites, and the work crews left the yard in a specific order. The fifty or more laundry workers were the first to leave. The men from the tailor and electrical shops departed next. The model shop workers then left, followed by the blacksmith shop workers. The model shop produced various wood products, including furniture, and the blacksmith shop performed the traditional duties of that trade, fashioning various products of metal. The clothing renovating crew and the cobbler shop employees were the next to leave. The war industry net and mat shop employees, along with the buoy detail, then departed. The net shop produced cargo nets for navy and merchant marine vessels, and the buoy detail serviced the buoys that held the anti-submarine net in place across the Golden Gate. The men in the mat shop fabricated deck matting for navy and merchant marine ships. The next group out was the incinerator crew, who manned the island incinerator. The freight handlers who worked on the dock and the clean-up crew were the last to leave. This group collected the garbage and swept the streets in the residential area of the island. The remaining prisoners were those assigned to duties in the cell-house, including the clothing and shower room, library, storeroom, front office, and the warden's passmen. There was usually a group of prisoners remaining behind for haircuts, interviews, and visits to the medical department. Finally, there was always a group of men listed as idle. These included men who were ill or who were not working for one reason or another. An accurate count was kept at all times, and immediately upon arrival at the shop or work station, each officer telephoned his tally to the armory officer. Many jobs required a change into work clothing once at the work site. Jobs such as those in the tailor shop did not involve heavy physical activity, and the inmates were permitted to work in coveralls.

While on the job, the inmates were closely supervised by both custodial officers and the shop foremen. The foremen were non-custodial civil service employees assigned to teach and supervise the technical phases of the work in the shops. At every work site, there were equipment and tools that could be used as deadly weapons, and those in authority never overlooked this. The risk of violence and death was always present, and none of us ever forgot it. Inmate surveillance was intense. The Alcatraz prisoner was not permitted to smoke on the job, but regular breaks were declared for rest, relaxation, and smoking. Many of the shops, such as the model shop and the net shop, contained highly inflammable materials, so the non-smoking regulation was as much of a safety measure as a disciplinary rule.

The officers in charge of work details kept an ongoing count of all inmates under their supervision. Every half hour, the officer made an official count of his detail and phoned the result to the armory officer. The alert officer kept a constant check on his crew at much shorter and irregular intervals. It was unwise for an officer to establish a regular routine, which the prisoners could observe and possibly take advantage of.

After a midmorning break, the inmates were back at work until a whistle blast signaled the end of the morning work period. Following a brief clean-up period, the inmates moved single file back up the hill. At the foot of the long concrete stairway leading to the yard, they passed through a metal detector similar to the one located at the dock. The detector could be set with such precision that even a safety pin would set off the warning buzzer. If the buzzer sounded, the inmate involved was searched by hand until the contraband was found. Often, inmates were randomly selected to be searched, even without setting off the alarm. Any inmate suspected of bringing in contraband that could not be detected by the electronic snitch-box was also searched here. One group of prisoners did not pass through the detector, but was always hand-searched. This was the handful of men who either wore medical garments containing metal or had metal embedded in their bodies from prior surgeries or shootouts. These men often acted as couriers of contraband and had to be watched with particular care. A second metal detector had to be traversed at the foot of the steps leading into the cell house.

The inmates walked immediately to their cells, where they changed into their trousers and shirts, washed up, and waited for the whistle signal to move into the mess hall. The noon meal generally consisted of soup, an entrée such as fish or meat, a vegetable, coffee, and huge stacks of bread. A favorite item of a great many of the men was gravy. When it was served they would pour it over bread and eat it as an entrée. Dessert, generally pie or ice cream, was served on Sunday. During the war years when meat was scarce, beans were often served as a meat substitute, and were eagerly received by most of the men.

Upon completion of the noon meal, the convicts returned to their cells for a smoke, quiet time, attendance to personal matters, and another count. When the count was correct, the convicts were permitted free time in their cells before returning to their afternoon work schedule. Amusing yet aggravating incidents often occurred during these general counts. At times, an error in the count would necessitate a second walk around the tier. If the delay was of some minutes, the convicts would set up a chorus to harass the officers. In addition, standing silently at his cell door cut into the convict's private time, and that was always grounds for complaint. Finally, the captain's whistle would signal a correct count and a mighty cheer mingled with boos would go up from the population.

The inmates would also cooperate with one another to disrupt the count. Often, when a new officer was counting a particular gallery, one of the convicts on that tier would hide under his bunk and the neophyte guard's count would be incorrect. He would be obliged to make a second trip, often with a chorus of boos and shouts making the recount even more difficult. To prolong the situation, a different inmate would hide during the second tally, causing the embarrassed and rattled guard to call out yet another incorrect total. Usually an experienced officer was sent up to the gallery to make the third count. By this time, however, the din was thunderous. When one of those episodes got underway, there was nothing the officers could do but let it run its course, and treat it as a humorous event. The unfortunate officer saw no humor, but he received a prison education he never forgot, and most likely never made a count error again.

At the conclusion of the count, inmates with special requests were released from their cells. The sick call line constituted the largest group. Some prisoners were released for interviews with the warden or associate warden, and others had to face the disciplinary board for violation of one or more prison regulations. Some had shoe and clothing problems and were released to the basement clothing room. After sick call and various personal activities were completed, another count was made, and the men returned to work. It was a repeat of the morning procedure, with the men filing out into the yard, then marching off to an afternoon of work.

The afternoon work procedure mirrored the morning, with the work day ending at 4:30 p.m. Thirty minutes later, the prisoners were marching out of their cells to go to the mess hall for the evening meal. At 5:30, supper was over and there was the final standing count marking the end of the day for the majority of the inmates. Kitchen workers and some of the cellhouse orderlies were still working, but most of the inmates were through. At this point, the cells were placed on deadlock position, which meant that the doors of the boxes containing the locking apparatus were locked for the night, with the key in the custody of the cellhouse officer. The day was also over for the day shift officers, who made their way to their island or mainland homes. It was the end of another tense watch, hopefully one without serious mishap, except perhaps for a fouled count or an abortive fight in the yard. But what of tomorrow? What sinister plans might be evolving in the minds of the

250 to 280 men who weren't going home that evening to family, friends or freedom? That was the challenge.

The prisoners still had four hours in their cells before lights out at 9:30. During this period they engaged in their quiet-time activities—art, music, reading, rolling cigarettes, tidying their cells, or simply lying in their bunks, relaxing and thinking. Thinking perhaps of their past days of freedom, or of the freedom that might come once more. Many, however, thought about society with hatred in their hearts, believing they had been treated unjustly. Some carried venomous grudges against fellow prisoners for actual or perceived offenses and plotted ways to "even the score." But the courts and law enforcement were the main targets of the malcontents. Injustice reigned supreme in the minds of many Alcatraz convicts. Their analysis, however, uniformly failed to account for their own injustice in robbing that bank, stealing that automobile, kidnapping that child, or killing that police officer who was protecting the lives and property of those being endangered. As I heard so often from the convicts, it was not their fault they were in Alcatraz. It was a crooked United States attorney, a lying witness, or their incompetent lawyer who was to blame. Regardless of the specific explanation, in nearly every case, "it was a bum rap."

While the inmate day had come to an end, a new custodial day was beginning for the evening watch, followed by the morning watch. Before morning, there would be several more counts while the inmates were in their cells. There was constant observation of the convicts. Throughout the day, there were fourteen official cell house counts, another seven verification counts in the shops and work sites, and numerous unofficial tallies in work areas. Throughout the night and early morning hours, the counting and observation continued.

Shaving was another of the inmates' evening activities. Three times a week, each inmate was given the opportunity to shave. On alternate evenings after lockup, the evening watch cellhouse officer issued each prisoner who wanted to shave his double-edged razor blade. One night, the men in B Block shaved, and the next night, it was C Block. At the conclusion of the shaving period, the blades were collected by the cellhouse officer and replaced on the board, which was stored at the main gate.

Also during the evening hours, the day's mail was delivered, and medical prescriptions from the hospital were distributed. An orderly was assigned to assist the cellhouse officer in the delivery of razor blades, mail, and medicine.

The inmates assigned to kitchen duty were the last to return to their cells. Their work day did not end until the evening meal cleanup and breakfast setup were complete. The kitchen crew was awakened an hour or two earlier than the main body of convicts to prepare breakfast. As a reward for this schedule, these men had the afternoons free to spend in the recreation yard or in their cells.

So went a typical inmate day on Alcatraz. Multiply it by hundreds or thousands and one has some idea of convict life. The vast majority of the population worked hard, harder than they ever did as free men. Most of them submitted and become institutionalized. But others did not, and were a constant danger to other inmates, the authorities, and themselves. Many suffered physical and mental torment from incarceration, and in the language of their convict contemporaries, went "stir crazy" or "blew their top."

Chapter VIII

Isolation and Solitary

In the free world, jails and prisons are built to hold those individuals who cannot adhere to constituted authority. In prison, there are also those who will not or cannot submit peaceably to authority, so for them there's a jail within a jail. At Alcatraz, that jail was D Block, the isolation section of the prison. Also known as the Treatment Unit or TU, it contained both isolation and solitary confinement cells. D Block was separated from the main cellhouse by a soundproof concrete wall, to isolate it as much as possible from the general population. The cells in isolation were larger than those in the main cellhouse, because the men in isolation were in their cells virtually twenty-four hours a day. In addition to the thirty-six standard isolation cells, D Block also contained six solitary confinement cells. These were the dark cells, also known as "the Hole." Inmates in solitary lived in total darkness and on a restricted diet. The only light they saw was twenty minutes three times a day at mealtime.

Serving time in isolation was dramatically different than doing time in general population. In isolation, the confinement was incredibly restricted, and there were very few privileges. Mail was delivered in the same manner as to other prisoners, and some of the long-term isolation residents were permitted to have visitors. Most could not, however. Books and magazines were permitted in isolation, but each piece of reading material was carefully checked page by page before being delivered to the prisoner. This was to prevent unauthorized messages being passed to D Block convicts.

D Block inmates ate all their meals in their cells. The food was wheeled into isolation in a large steam cart from the kitchen, and the isolation officer made up the food trays for the convicts. He was assisted by an inmate orderly, also a D Block resident, who delivered the food trays to the individual cells. All utensils were carefully accounted for after each meal.

Inmates were placed in isolation for numerous reasons. An escape attempt landed a prisoner in isolation for months, or even years. Fighting, drunkenness, repeated disobedience, possession of certain types of contraband such as weapons, repeatedly wasting food, destruction of property, and other serious infractions could result in confinement in D Block. Often, inmates who served a stint in solitary would continue to be held in isolation after being released from the Hole. Most of the men confined in isolation were convicts who had shown by their previous conduct that they were still incorrigible after arriving at Alcatraz. In addition, some prisoners were placed in isolation for their own safety, occasionally at their own request. These included sociopaths, psychopaths, and other mentally unstable men who were likely to injure others or be injured. Suicidal inmates were in D Block, where they could be closely monitored.

Serving time in solitary was a temporary, punitive measure, and resulted from violation of any number of prison regulations. Whether or not an inmate was sent to solitary depended upon the seriousness of the offense and his previous record. Bureau of Prisons regulations prohibited an inmate from being held in solitary longer than nineteen consecutive days. There were rare instances when the violation was so aggravated and the inmate's record so bad that a prisoner would be confined for nineteen days, released for a day, then put back in solitary for several more days.

The solitary cells were constructed in two sections. The outer door was solid steel and led to a small vestibule outside the cell itself. This solid door was insulated around the edges so no light or sound could penetrate the doorway. The inner door was barred and covered with a fine screen. An opening in the barred door permitted the officer to pass food and utensils through to the convict. The cell was furnished with a toilet, a steel bunk mounted on the wall, and a small sink/drinking fountain combination. There was a recessed light in the rear wall of the cell, which was turned on at mealtime only. At all other times, the cell was totally dark with not even a pinpoint of light entering. The inmate was not permitted to have bedding during the day, but in the evening he was given a mattress and two blankets. The floor of the cell was covered with brown linoleum. The inmate was furnished toilet tissue, but no other toilet articles. During the time he was in solitary, the man did not shave, brush his teeth, comb his hair, or take a bath.

One of the solitary cells was a "stripped cell." This cubicle had no fixtures of any type, and only a hole in the floor for urination and defecation. It was here that the truly uncontrollable convict was placed. A trip to the stripped cell usually followed the inmate's destruction of the fixtures in a regular solitary cell or some other act of total and wanton destruction. It was the most severe confinement that existed on Alcatraz.

An inmate was placed in solitary or isolation following a hearing of the Disciplinary Board. This consisted of the associate warden, the captain or one of the lieutenants, and one or more officers available for such duty. The charge was read from the report, or "shot," as the inmates referred to it. Upon conclusion of the reading of the report, the prisoner was given an opportunity to explain his side. There was usually a discussion of the case among the board members, unless the inmate presented no defense. The associate warden generally suggested the disciplinary action, and the officers either concurred with or disputed the suggestion. In almost all cases, there was complete concurrence, although at times I was involved in cases where officers made favorable presentations on behalf of an inmate. Over the years, I saw some harsh penalties meted out, but no injustice. Virtually every case I saw involved repeated violations, or a single but serious infraction. Most of the time, the hearing was a formality because the offensive conduct was so egregious. Very few officers put any inmate on report for anything but serious or repeated violations. Minor infractions were handled by warning and lecturing the offender.

After it was decided that an inmate was to be placed in solitary, he was ushered through the heavy steel door to D Block. Here, he was stripped of all his regular clothing. He was searched thoroughly, including such places as his hair, between his fingers and toes, in his mouth, under his feet, and finally his crotch and rectum. These precautions were taken to prevent the inmate from secreting contraband, or anything with which he could do bodily harm to himself while in solitary. He was then given clean underwear, a clean pair of coveralls, and a pair of soft cloth slippers.

Although the days of bread and water while in solitary had passed, the restricted diet the prisoner received was anything but appealing. Federal prison regulations dictated the following solitary confinement menu:

Breakfast	1 bowl of coffee
	4 slices of bread
Lunch	1 bowl of soup
	4 slices of bread
Dinner	1 bowl of tea or coffee
	1 serving of lettuce salad
	4 slices of bread

While in solitary, a man received a full meal every third day at noon, the same meal served to the general population.

At the conclusion of his stay in solitary, the prisoner was permitted to shave and bathe. If he went back to the general population, he had some or all of his privileges restored, depending upon the conditions of his case. There was little uniformity in the handling of solitary and isolation cases. Each was decided entirely on its own merits, taking into consideration the facts and the convict's prior record.

The effect solitary confinement had on the inmates was as varied as the number of inmates confined there. Some would be broken in a few hours or days and would readily agree to conform to the rules. Others seemed to do their time as easily in the Hole as any other place in the prison. Most men were eager to come out, and welcomed the opportunity for a shower and a shave. While solitary confinement was a severe punishment, it was meted out judiciously and reserved for the worst offenders and the most serious offenses. The threat of such harsh treatment was needed to control some of those at Alcatraz, and when the threat was not enough, there was the real thing. Solitary almost always accomplished its goal.

D Block, the isolation section of the prison. Bottom tier shower cell shown immediately to the right of the stairs. Solitary cells—the Hole—were at the far end of bottom tier.

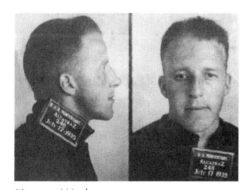

Harmon Wayley

Wayley and Dainard, kidnappers for ransom of the child of the wealthy Weyerhauser family in Washington state, who were long-time residents of D Block.

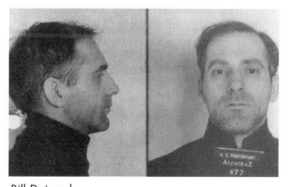

Bill Dainard

Isolation was a more long-term status, and housed the problem prisoners. These were usually the most incorrigible among the incorrigibles. A brief description of the men in isolation during my exposure to D Block illustrates my point:

James Lucas and **Rufus "Whitey" Franklin,** who participated in an abortive escape attempt in 1938. During the attempt, officer Royal Cline was bludgeoned to death.

 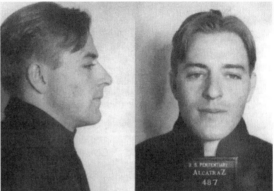

Fred Hunter   Harold Brest

Fred Hunter, Harold Brest, and **Floyd Hamilton,** who were part of an escape attempt in 1943 in which one of their number, James Boarman, was shot to death while attempting to swim to freedom.

Henri Young, a two-time murderer who took active part in a daring escape attempt in 1939. In a letter to the attorney general of the United States requesting that Young be transferred from McNeil Island to Alcatraz, the convict was described by United States Attorney J. M. Simpson as "the worst and most dangerous criminal with whom I have ever dealt."

Robert Stroud, dubbed the "Birdman of Alcatraz" by Hollywood, spent much of his lengthy stay on Alcatraz in isolation.

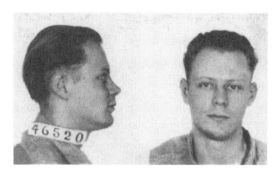

Burton Phillips viciously attacked Warden Johnston in the dining hall on September 24, 1937, rendering him unconscious and inflicting serious injuries. Phillips spent several years thereafter in isolation.

Robert Stroud, the inappropriately named "Birdman of Alcatraz" (he never had birds at Alcatraz), a two-time killer whose death sentence had been commuted to life in isolation by President Woodrow Wilson.

Joseph Cretzer, Sam Shockley, Arnold Kyle, and **Lloyd Barkdoll,** who attempted to escape in 1941 after overpowering an officer and a civilian employee in the mat shop. Cretzer and Shockley were also part of the bloody breakout attempt of 1946.

Several convicts who would not work. They preferred isolation to working.

Burton Phillips, who in 1937 beat Warden Johnston into insensibility, erroneously believing that the warden was withholding his correspondence from the court.

John Richard Bayless, a convicted bank robber who escaped from his work site one foggy afternoon and attempted to swim to San Francisco. He was captured and subsequently tried in federal court for attempted escape. During his trial, he broke away from the U.S. Marshal who was guarding him and again attempted to escape. Captured and retried, he received a thirty-year sentence for escape in addition to the forty-five years he was already serving for robbery.

Two kidnappers, one who threatened to kill anyone who got in his way, and the other suspected of designing and attempting to build a pair of guns in the machine shop.

Several psychopathic convicts, who were either afraid of other inmates or threats to other prisoners.

A violent sexual pervert, who could not get along with other inmates in general population.

A sexual deviate handy with a shiv, who had been convicted of killing one inmate and was suspected of stabbing several others. He was confined in isolation because he was considered a menace to those in the general population.

There were others in isolation, all similar to those described. The faces changed, but the type of inmate remained constant. Occasionally, inmates were released from isolation into general population, often with some degree of success, and at other times, to the sorrow and despair of many. There was no proven means of determining when a particular prisoner was rehabilitated to the point that it was safe to return him to general population. This decision was made all the more difficult because the diabolical inmate minds were able to devise ways of convincing the authorities that they were ready for return to the main cellhouse when they really weren't.

The convict in isolation shaved twice each week if he so desired. A razor blade board like that in the main cellhouse was maintained for D Block, and the isolation officer handed out the blades and shaving materials. Unlike the main cellhouse, however, none of the shaving equipment was permitted in the cells, but was stored in a locker maintained by the D Block officer. Potentially suicidal inmates were given an assembled razor from which the blade could not be removed. Even with this precaution, there were still several suicide attempts using razors.

While movies and recorded music were available as recreation for inmates in the general population, prisoners in isolation got neither. Except for a few short periods, the inmates in isolation were in their cells continuously. Brief periods in the recreation yard and weekly showers were the only exceptions. Yard time of an hour and a half was permitted for some prisoners two days a week. Depending upon their situation, some prisoners got less time in the yard, and some got none. During yard periods, they were permitted to play handball or merely walk about. They had no access to horseshoes or softball bats, or any other recreation devices that could be used as weapons. Care was taken to keep known enemies from being in the yard at the same time. During recreation periods, additional armed guards were stationed on the wall to discourage even the most daring convict from attempting to escape or attacking a fellow inmate. During the entire time the isolation prisoners were in the yard, the isolation officer was with them, making D Block was one of the most dangerous custodial assignments in the prison.

Despite all the care that was exercised, violence still occurred. Once, as the inmates moved through the metal detector, one of them laid open another's scalp with a horseshoe he had surreptitiously picked up in the corner of the equipment closet and concealed under his coat. Some weeks later, the same two prisoners mistakenly ended up in the yard at the same time, and the horseshoe victim gashed his assailant's face with the broken half of a small medicine bottle he had somehow managed to obtain. Fights in the isolation recreation yard did not occur often, but the risk of serious trouble was always there.

The food was the same as that served on the main line, although one heard more complaints about the food in isolation than in the general population. The D Block prisoners complained a lot about everything, no doubt because they had little else to do. The evening meal on bean day was the favorite meal, and the Sunday pie was a major culinary event.

The use of chessboards was permitted in isolation, and virtually every afternoon, there would be one or more chess matches in progress. The matches were played with each player having two chess sets on his board. The squares on the board were numbered and the inmates called out their moves to one another. Each player would move his opponent's pieces in accordance with the move called out by his adversary. Inevitably, the calling out of the chess moves interfered with some inmate's reading or sleeping, and verbal hostility resulted. The chess players were never deterred, and the games went on.

Because of their inactivity, a number of the convicts in isolation worked hard to keep themselves physically fit. They regularly did sit-ups and pushups, either on the floor of the cell or using the bars of the door of the cell as supports for their exercises. Others, however, just relaxed, ate, slept, and got fat. Some prisoners actually seemed to thrive on the isolation inactivity.

The men in isolation received even less news of the outside world than those in the general population. Consequently, they were eager for any bit of information an officer might disclose, and most of the officers willingly passed along information regarding the war. During my assignment in D Block, a bright young convict took it upon himself to fill the news void in D Block in a clever and entertaining way. I never knew his real name, but he was known to officers and inmates alike as Bingo. He was one of the most likeable convicts in the institution, and I never learned what misconduct had landed him in isolation. During his yard period twice a week, he went to a corner of the yard beneath the guard station on the wall and received whatever information he could from the officer on duty there. Immediately after all the inmates were back in their cells he would call out in a voice loud enough to be heard throughout D Block:

"Station B-I-N-G-O is now on the air broadcastin' all the news of the day. It is reported that the German Luftwaffe made a bombing strike on London last night with only minimal loss of English life, but a number of German planes were shot down....." and so on. His broadcast would go on for several minutes, and I'm sure he made up a few of the stories as he went along. The inmates would listen intently as Bingo broadcasted the news, and when he signed off, there was always a mighty cheer and a hearty round of applause. It was an event all of us in isolation looked forward to.

During mealtime, the isolation officer rather than the inmate orderly served food to prisoners in solitary. It was part of the punishment to keep the prisoner in total solitary confinement and away from all other inmates, and of course, there was a possibility that another inmate might pass contraband to the man in solitary. Little or no conversation took place between the officer and the inmate during the meal service. When the solitary cells were opened during mealtime, the other D Block convicts set up a chorus of supportive shouting:

"Hang in there, old buddy, we're all pullin' for you."

"How you doin' down there, Charlie? Hope you get outta' there soon."

"Good luck bad-ass. Hang tough down there."

With such words of encouragement ringing in his ears, the solitary cell resident would eat his solitary meal then return to the blackness of his steel box.

Attempts were periodically made to smuggle contraband materials to the men in solitary. I recall one such incident while I was working as the isolation officer. Salt was not usually provided to those in solitary, but on this occasion, the inmate in the Hole asked for salt. I called to my mess orderly for the salt shaker and it was almost as if the orderly was waiting to deliver the salt to me. Suspicious, I unscrewed the top of the salt shaker. Inside the shaker was an entire smoking unit. Wrapped tightly so it fit inside a two- or three-inch-high salt shaker was a bag of tobacco, cigarette papers, and matches. I removed the contraband as the prisoner watched, then asked him, "Do you still want the salt?"

"Hell, no, Boss. You knew all along I didn't want salt. You're just too damned careful. All I wanted was a smoke."

The interesting thing about the episode was that rather than antipathy, my conduct was greeted with respect. It was part of the prison game, and in this instance I had won, and the convict willingly admitted it. Not all prisoners would have reacted that way, and from many I would have received an abusive line of obscenity.

Just as with the general population, isolation inmates delighted in creating discomfort for the officers, and used every device available to them to do so. During the collection of silverware and serving vessels, a spoon or bowl would often be held out for a short time, but long enough to make it inconvenient for the officer. Before long, the orderly would come down with the missing item, for a missing utensil would mean a general shakedown of the entire block, and no one wanted that. I used the mess orderly to prevent such little inconveniences. I would make it politely but firmly clear to each orderly that if he wished to retain his job it was his personal responsibility to return with every serving item and every piece of silverware from every cell. He delivered them and he had to return with them, or he lost his job. I never had any trouble with lost items.

Given the extreme care exercised, one would not expect that contraband material would make its way into the isolation block, but it did. At one time, several inmates were discovered to possess bits of files and hack saw blades, which they were using to cut the steel walls of their cells. The plan was to get atop the block and out the corridor. These bits of prison contraband had been smuggled into D Block in the hollowed-out handle of a broom.

In another instance, one of the officers in the main cellhouse on routine patrol decided to peek through the window in the door to D Block. It was almost never done, but on this occasion, he looked in and observed an inmate filing a bar to the gun gallery. He had made quite a large cut in a bar before he was discovered. The inmate was a D Block orderly, who was supposed to be sweeping the floor while the isolation officer was working up on one of the tiers. The block was given a thorough shakedown, and the file was found.

Both the kidnappers involved in the famous Weyerhauser case were in D Block at the time I was working there. Harmon Wayley and William Dainard kidnapped the young child of the Weyerhauser family in Washington state in the 1930s and held the youngster for ransom. The family had amassed great wealth in the lumber and shipping industry. Occasionally, one of the Weyerhauser lumber schooners would go in or out the Golden Gate, and the inmates on the upper tiers who could see the bay would yell out, "Hey, Bill and Harmon, there goes one of your boats all loaded down with lumber." Bill and Harmon did not appreciate the comments, nor did they respond.

Occasionally the entire isolation block would engage in a vocal uprising. Anything could set it off, and the noise would be deafening. It could last for many hours, and, on occasion, would spread to the main cellhouse. The isolation block was generally soundproof, but when twenty-five or thirty men began yelling, screaming, and banging their metal drinking cups on the bars as loudly as they could, some of the sound came through. The result could be the upsetting of the equanimity of the general population, and the entire prison would erupt in an explosion of sound. It didn't happen often, but when it did, the ruckus could be heard all over the island, and probably by nearby boats and ships in the bay.

One evening, the isolation inmates began a vocal riot, which went on for hours. While it didn't spread to the main cellhouse, it was a deafening experience for anyone in D Block. In time, the officer on watch in isolation could contain himself no longer. He unrolled the firehose, turned on the water and drenched the inmates one by one with the salt water normally used to fight fires. The clamor ceased at once, but the officer's conduct was considered unacceptable by the prison administration. The duty lieutenant responded, and the overzealous officer was relieved. He was later reprimanded and transferred to another institution. Most of the custodial staff was in total sympathy with him and we congratulated him on doing what most of us wanted to do, but never had the courage, or foolhardiness, to do.

Isolation was an abnormal part of an abnormal institution. The main prison was strange, and D Block was stranger still. The work of the officer in isolation was stressful and dangerous, and most of the officers did not welcome the assignment. The constant chatter, foul language, and egotistical harangues of the men confined there were viewed by some on the custodial force as a form of torture. The everlasting diatribes and invectives hurled at all in authority, from the president of the United States to the warden and his officers, was, at best, unpleasant. Danger lurked at all times. It could come in the form of an attack by one inmate on another, an attempt at suicide, or even an attack on a supervising officer. You never relaxed, you never rested, and you never turned your back. It was always with a sigh of relief when the next shift arrived, and you were off-duty.

Chapter IX

Contraband and Shakedown

A vital security concern in any prison is the presence of contraband, and it was a constant problem at Alcatraz. The search or shakedown for unauthorized material was a major part of life in the island prison. There were two types of contraband: materials prohibited for disciplinary reasons and items that endangered the lives and safety of individuals, either custodial or inmate. The former included unauthorized knick knacks, rugs, clothing, and unauthorized food. The items of major concern, however, were deadly weapons such as knives, cudgels, stabbing devices of all kinds, garrotes, and an array of deadly devices.

Every officer in charge of a shop or work detail was trained to be alert for illegal articles. In addition, every area occupied by prisoners was given periodic shakedowns, minute inspections designed to locate unauthorized items. Inmates were searched several times each day, either physically or by electromagnetic detectors. Passage into certain areas was not permitted until the inmate had submitted to a search of his person. Pockets, handkerchiefs, matchboxes, and all personal items were carefully examined, and as a result of these multiple searches, contraband was held to a minimum.

The greatest concentration of illicit material was in the cellhouse, and this was the center of shakedown activity. It was customary to have several extra officers on shakedown duty on Saturday and Sunday, as no shops were in operation during the weekend and most of the prisoners spent their time in the recreation yard. That made it easy to search both the work area and the cells. It was preferable to conduct shakedowns in the absence of the inmates. Specific tiers of cells would be selected and each cell on that tier was meticulously searched. While a few of the officers were a bit slipshod in their approach to the task, most officers conducted rigorous searches. Normally, inmates did not hide deadly weapons in their cells because of the ease of identification. A deadly weapon found in a cell got the occupant an immediate trip to the Hole, so these items were usually hidden in public areas not associated with any one convict. But the cells yielded a plethora of forbidden items.

Many inmates had a mania for civilian underwear, which would be stolen from the officers' laundry in the work area. Others possessed stolen doilies, napkins, towels, et cetera, with which they decorated their shelf or their small folding desks. The shakedown officers confiscated these bits of illegal material, and the inmate involved was often placed on report.

Blackened drinking cups always drew the attention of the authorities. A sooty cup (often with wires attached to it) indicated that cooking had taken place in the cell. It could have been during the night or, in the case of idle inmates, during the long dreary day. Coffee was the most common menu item produced by these in-cell chefs. Coffee was smuggled into the cellhouse from the kitchen by an inmate or his friends. Fires were built of wadded-up toilet tissue and the coffee was brewed over the fire. Occasionally, the java brewer was caught in the act, but this was rare. Many were the nights that I made my rounds along the quiet galleries and smelled the aroma of brewing coffee. I never went searching for the culprit, for the offense was harmless and fairly common. Most officers shared my views and ignored the practice.

Decorative boxes made in the shops constituted one of the most common forms of contraband. Some boxes were allowed by special permission of the captain and associate warden, but not all boxes were permitted. Unauthorized items were seized and placed in the contraband heap. Approved boxes were made to hold the wooden cards and dominoes used during recreation periods in the yard. Other boxes were used to hold rolled cigarettes, art supplies, or other personal items. Some of these containers were independent works of art in their design, construction, and decoration. But anything not previously approved was contraband, regardless of its beauty.

A far more serious type of contraband was the array of deadly weapons that commonly appeared during shakedowns. Knives, daggers, stilettos, and various stabbing weapons were often fabricated from kitchen utensils, large nails, and virtually any piece of metal, glass, or heavy plastic. These vicious tools were honed to razor sharpness at the edges or points, and handles were fashioned using cord, leather, cloth, or other material, producing highly effective killing instruments. When an inmate stabbing occurred, it was nearly always with one of these lethal homemade weapons. Cudgel-type weapons were often cloth bags containing stones, or socks filled with cakes of soap. Both made effective blackjacks.

One of these convict-made knives was used in an attack on a well-known inmate who ultimately died from his wounds. True to the prison code of silence, he never divulged the name of his killer even though he was advised by the treating physican that his wound was fatal. The murder weapon was not found, and the authorities, including the FBI, were in a quandary. One morning a couple of days after the killing, a cellhouse orderly approached me seeking advice.

"Boss, what should I do, I found the knife that was used in the killin'. I found it when I was cleaning up the blood on the gallery."

"Tell me where the knife is," I said, "and I'll pass the information along to the associate warden. He'll come and talk to you, and nobody but the three of us will ever know." This was done, and in time, the knife became a valuable piece of evidence in the conviction of the killer without any help from the murdered man.

If an inmate was in his cell during a shakedown, it was necessary for him to step out while the search was conducted. Most of the convicts did so grudgingly, but some did it with a laugh and a wisecrack. Naturally, any inmate who observed the searches shared this information with his contemporaries who were not in their cells, advising them that their cell had been raided by the cops. Those who had illegal contraband immediately looked for it when they returned to their cells to determine if they had been "busted." These observers would also identify the officers who busted them so reprisals could be taken if the convicts involved so desired and could carry it off.

Reprisals usually took the form of lost personal items from the laundry, torn sheets, torn shirts, and other forms of damage impossible to trace. Laundry retaliation included dress shirts returned with one sleeve missing or a huge hole in the front. Such reprisals were directed not only toward shakedown officers, but to any officer against whom an inmate might harbor a grudge. If the inmate wasn't working in the laundry himself, he would have a friend carry out his acts of revenge. If he had no friends in the laundry, he might hire someone to accomplish it for him. When it came to making life difficult for an officer, the convicts cooperated fully with one another.

A portable metal detector was often employed in cell shakedown, and would be wheeled along the gallery from cell to cell. During the inspection of the cell one of the officers would operate the portable snitch box while others passed mattresses, bedding, pillows, and other items through its electrical field. Metal items could not escape detection by the highly sensitive machine.

Consumption of liquor had been a significant part of the fast lives most of the prisoners led during their years of freedom. Not surprisingly, therefore, a continuing form of contraband in the prison was home brew, and the custodial force was ever watchful for batches of the illegal nectar. The bakery and kitchen, with their inventories of yeast, malt syrup, and other prime ingredients, were the most common distilling venues on the island. Liquor was found in the shops as well. Anything that would ferment was employed to brew a drink with a kick: fruit peels, fruit pits, fruit of all kinds, and (of course) sugar. Home brew was made in jugs, cans, virtually any container available. On one occasion during a special shakedown in the laundry, a huge cache of brew was discovered in a pair of rubber boots hanging on the wall. It became an ongoing contest between inmates and officers, with the former brewing and hiding, and the latter searching and destroying. At one point, the inmates were winning the game and for many months, homemade "elixir of joy" appeared from an unknown source. The foolproof container turned out to be a fire extinguisher in the kitchen. The fire retardant chemicals had been removed, the container cleaned, and the fire extinguisher became a still. The hose attached to the unit served as the dispenser. Everything went perfectly until it became time to test and service the extinguisher; then the cons were busted.

If not discovered and allowed to ferment to completion, the home brew was remarkably potent. In addition to becoming quite intoxicated, most of the inmates who tried the brew became violently ill. They rarely exercised restraint in their consumption, and after years of abstinence, their stomachs couldn't handle the shock of the primitive concoctions. So, in addition to king-sized hangovers, there was usually a short-term illness.

In addition to the cellhouse, shakedowns were conducted in other areas of the prison. The shops and work areas were constantly being inspected, often on the basis of tips from informers, but also as part of prison routine. All manner of contraband was found during these inspections. Not surprisingly, the kitchen and bakery were frequent shakedown targets. Shop, kitchen, and bakery shakedowns were almost always conducted on weekends or evenings, in the absence of the inmate work force.

Cell and window bars received particular attention. Officers would pass a thin blade along the bars searching for saw or file cuts. If a depression was found, further probing occasionally disclosed putty, paint or soap, which was employed to conceal a cut. The bars on the outside windows were tapped vigorously with a hard rubber mallet. Bars producing a dull, loose ring had probably been tampered with, and were more thoroughly inspected. Cell bars, too, were frequently tested with the rubber mallet.

It was a seemingly innocuous bit of contraband that led to one the largest cases of illegal smuggling in Alcatraz history. The inmate involved was Louis Fleish, a former member of the notorious Purple Gang of Detroit. His was truly an Alcatraz family; his two older brothers, Harry and Sam, both also served time on The Rock. While passing from the shops to the cellhouse for the noon meal, Fleish, who was considered a model prisoner, was detected smuggling a hand-made unauthorized box into his cell. While the inmates were eating, a group of officers searched Fleish's cell. They found several packages of chewing gum, commercially made cigarettes, candy, a nearly full box of cigars, and slightly less than twenty dollars in cash. When asked to explain the extraordinary array of smuggled items, Fleish refused to identify the source of the contraband. He was sent immediately to solitary and later placed in isolation. He remained in isolation for several years, but never revealed the name of the smuggler. There was widespread concern as to who could have been the source of such an overwhelming supply of illicit material. Clearly, the smuggler was an employee, either an officer, a clerk, or one of the civilian shop foremen. The over-

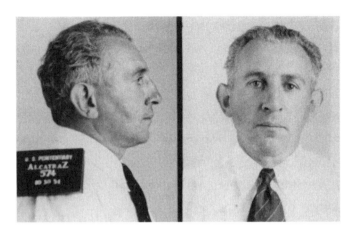

Louis Fleish, center of the most sensational case of illegal smuggling in Alcatraz history. Fleisch never identified the smuggler, and as a result, spent years in isolation.

riding question at the time was whether this was everything, or was something more dangerous hidden somewhere else in the prison? A great deal of suspicion swirled about the island, along with much secret finger-pointing. Despite an extensive investigation, the responsible party was never identified. The investigation was limited to the Alcatraz staff, and the matter was never reported to the bureau's Washington office. It remained a quiet Alcatraz scandal, and Fleish paid dearly for his involvement. I don't know if Louie ever got out of isolation.

The Louie Fleish case was an anomaly in the world of convict conduct, and the only case of its kind with which I am familiar. It also demonstrated something about the character of Louie Fleish. Most inmates would immediately identify the smuggler in the hope of lessening their own penalty. Fleish never did that.

Almost without exception, all contraband plotters were identified, with dire results for both inmate and employee. On one such occasion, the officer in question was brought to trial in federal court and sentenced to prison. He was relatively new to prison work when he was assigned to isolation, evening watch. He was a softhearted young man, and somehow the condition of D Block got a hold on him. Throughout the course of several weeks, this foolish young man carried several loads of contraband into D Block in his lunch box. Before the plot was uncovered, he had brought in several pints of whiskey, gum, snuff, and several Benzedrine inhalers. The Benzedrine-soaked cotton in the inhalers was removed and swallowed, providing a short-term high to the imbiber. A tip regarding the smuggling came from one of the inmate stool pigeons, and the hunt was on. One

Sunday afternoon, a large number of off-duty officers were called in to conduct the search. The officers were briefed, and each man was assigned a specific area to search. Prior to the search, the officer in charge of D Block turned off all the water to the cells so nothing could be flushed down the toilets. The shakedown was sudden and thorough, and in a matter of minutes, every cell had been meticulously searched. In addition to the anticipated contraband, considerable amounts of other illegal items were found. The officer in question was confronted when he reported for his evening shift. Faced with the overwhelming evidence, he confessed to his part in the affair. There was no code of silence in that case, and the officer readily incriminated all the prisoners involved.

On another occasion, the mail censor noted a large number of photographs arriving in the mail of one of the inmate artists. He would paint portraits from these photos and send the artwork to his family. The censor observed that more photographs were arriving than portraits being sent out. He instigated an investigation, which revealed that an officer was smuggling the artwork out of the prison, shipping it for a fee to customers around the country, and realizing a profit. Since his conduct did not constitute a felony under then-existing law, he was not charged criminally. He was, however, fired, ending forever his career in law enforcement.

Another bizarre incident involved an officer carrying out uncensored letters for an inmate, then mailing them to the addressees. Most of the letters went to the inmate's family, but some were sent to friends. The officer received money from the family of the prisoner for his services. In time, the officer reconsidered his conduct and sent the money back to those who had paid him. The inmate involved was either not satisfied with the explanation or angry because the officer was breaking off his illicit service, and threatened to expose the smuggler. A second officer then became involved to verify that the money had been repaid in a misguided effort to help the first officer. The result of this incredible folly was the discharge of the first officer and the forced retirement of the second.

I never understood how men under oath to serve the public and the federal Bureau of Prisons could lower themselves to the depths necessary to plot with the human dregs confined at Alcatraz. For an officer to think he was establishing a relationship of friendship by such illegal conduct was absurd, for they would turn on you in an instant if it was in their best interest to do so. Fortunately, there were very few such officers, but in my view, one was too many.

Chapter X

Mental Health in Prison

Freedom is the natural state of animal life. All animals, including man, resist captivity, and this resistance manifests itself in various ways. Wild animals fight viciously when their freedom is threatened. Social wrongdoers react similarly. There is often a violent response to the attempted capture by law enforcement officials. There may be attempts to escape once an offender is captured. The trial of a criminal case is a fight, conducted in a peaceful rather than a violent setting. The guilty criminal defendant can lose his freedom for years, and the resulting imprisonment may offer little that is good or encouraging. Incarceration is an unnatural human condition and those confined often do not endure captivity successfully. In addition to a total loss of freedom and little to look forward to, one's contemporaries in prison are bad and violent men. Confinement for long periods is harsh and often produces extreme reactions. Many convicts seek revenge, attempt to escape, grow morbid, or withdraw. Suicide attempts, some of which are successful, are not uncommon. Lengthy sentences alone are often enough to cause some men to lose touch with reality, and there are all manner of emotional, psychological, and psychiatric responses to rigid imprisonment.

While our training at Alcatraz did not include instruction in psychiatry or psychology, the mental stability of the prisoners was a phase of the work with which we had to deal. Although we were basically custodians of dangerous and violent men, most of us became adept at discerning signs of abnormal inmate behavior. The refusal of food, a quarrelsome attitude toward his fellow prisoners, the loss of interest in his surroundings, withdrawal or depression, requests for release from his job, and a number of other outward signs often signaled mental deterioration. In addition, there were those who feigned mental disturbance in the hope of some self-gain or possible hospitalization. And there were always those who sought transfer to the medical facility in Springfield, Missouri, where the custodial conditions were less restrictive.

Many convicts sought medical care as an outlet for their confined emotions or to get attention. Daily sick call included a significant number of the "regulars," plus a few prisoners who only appeared in the sick line if they really had something wrong with them. The hypochondriacs usually required little more than a couple of all-purpose capsules or a bottle of rhubarb and soda. A number of these continually ill prisoners developed a significant medical education, and would arrive at the hospital with a complete list of symptoms and a diagnosis. If the doctor did not agree with their diagnosis and recommended treatment, he could expect to see them at the next sick call. These patients were the curse of the Alcatraz medical staff. They never got well and they never died.

Another troublesome patient was the paranoiac. This individual constantly complained that the authorities were persecuting him. He believed that his mail was being withheld, that he was restricted for violations for which others were merely reprimanded, and that the officers were picking on him. Since he was not sufficiently afflicted to be sent to Springfield, he remained basically an insoluble problem for the Alcatraz medical staff.

The uncooperative inmate was another neurotic or psychotic type with which we had to deal. This convict didn't want to work. He didn't seem too concerned about his restrictions, and was content to stay in his cell, leaving it only for meals. One such individual had never accepted a job during the six or seven years he had been confined on Alcatraz. During the day, he repeatedly washed his handkerchiefs and socks in his cell sink and hung them on strings to dry. He answered sullenly when spoken to, and refused to be drawn into a conversation. Some men were intermittently cooperative and uncooperative. They might go along for weeks on a particular job, doing well and working hard. Then suddenly, for no apparent reason, they would withdraw to their cells and refuse to come out except for meals.

Over time, many of us developed some psychological expertise through on-the-job training. You learned the psychological ploys the inmates played and how to beat them at their own games. Without question, the most outstanding practical prison psychologist was our associate warden, Ed Miller. While his formal education was limited, his long years of supervising all kinds of convicts had made him a master at the art of managing men. He instinctively knew when to use cajolery with an inmate, when to bluster, when to explode, and when to use stealth. While certainly not loved by the inmates, "Jughead," as he was referred to by the prisoners, was highly respected by the entire population, and to some extent feared. The fear was not fostered by brutality, because that was not part of Jughead's makeup. They feared him because he was fair and always meant what he said and said what he meant. That combination was often difficult for the Alcatraz convict.

The violent "stir crazies" presented a serious and dangerous problem during their outbursts. These men expressed their psychoses through violent physical conduct during which they destroyed property and often injured themselves. Dealing with these explosive rampages was always a matter of competing considerations. Should you try to overpower the raging prisoner, with possible injury to the prisoner and officers, or let the violence run its course? If property damage was the primary risk, and it didn't appear as though the prisoner would injure himself, the tirade was usually allowed to run its course. Once he calmed down, the "psycho" might remain calm for months or even years. But most gave repeat performances.

One of the more memorable cases of psychotic violence involved an inmate I knew well. Lloyd Barkdoll, serving a life sentence, was a powerfully built young man capable of performing amazing feats of strength. During one of his fits, the thirty-four old Barkdoll bent the steel bunk in his cell in half and jammed it into the cell door with such force that it was impossible to open the door. After he had thrown everything out of his cell, including books, clothing, torn-up mattress, bedding, and all his personal effects, he quietly announced, "Okay, Boss, I'm all done now, so you can throw me in the Hole." After the maintenance people managed to disengage the bunk from the cell door and get the door open, that's where Barkdoll went. It was not a long stay, but long enough for him to reflect upon the point that such conduct was unacceptable regardless of his mental condition.

Barkdoll had a violent history, including attempting escape from Alcatraz in

1941, and was always considered dangerous. After his tour in solitary, he was returned to the general population and soon became a model prisoner. He was ultimately assigned to the kitchen, then promoted to the officers' dining room. He became a leader among the inmates, and enjoyed a high degree of respect from his contemporaries. He was also the moving force in the establishment of the convict orchestra, The Rock Islanders. I always liked Barkdoll, and we got along well even during his stormy period. Married and devoted to his wife, he loved to talk about family life, and enjoyed hearing about my family. Unfortunately, this seemingly healthy and virile man died from a heart attack in 1950. It was a sad way for his sentence to end, for he had turned his life around and was thinking seriously about possible transfer and parole.

An inmate whose time was spent almost entirely in isolation illustrated the combination of a violent personality hidden behind a quiet, somber facade. The man's original sentence was not long, but while serving time in another federal prison, he murdered an inmate. After coming to Alcatraz, he got into trouble and ended up in isolation. In isolation he was quiet, rational, and courteous to the officers at all times. Based on his excellent conduct in D Block, his request for yard time was granted. During his first minutes of yard time he viciously attacked a fellow inmate, whom he barely knew. He was quickly subdued and hustled into the Hole. After he came out of solitary, I asked him about his bizarre conduct.

"Oh, hell, Boss, I didn't care about getting yard privileges, I just wanted to beat the hell out of that guy."

During our discussions, he was rational and candid in describing himself and his conduct: "Sure, Boss, I'm psycho, I'm crazy as hell. Can't you tell?"

Another case with which I dealt was an example of how the terrifying violence of prison can take a toll on human life. The prisoner involved had been the victim of a vicious beating and slashing at the hands of two other inmates in the kitchen. He suffered the dreadful attack for having accidentally witnessed homosexual activity between his assailants. After recovering from his wounds, he was placed in isolation at his own request. After a period of contemplative quiet in isolation, he suddenly became violent and had to be transferred to a locked-down cell in the hospital. He developed deep-seated feelings of paranoia and claimed to be the victim of persecution.

He contended that the officers and hospital personnel were attempting to poison him and he refused to eat. He was ultimately placed in loose restraints. One Sunday, a call for help came from the hospital, and several of us were dispatched to assist the officer in charge of the hospital and the medical staff. When we arrived, the convict was in a frenzied, maniacal state, screaming, cursing, and flailing about, threatening all present, including the doctor. Having been restrained, he was denied bathroom privileges, and upon our arrival, we were threatened by the raving inmate brandishing a portable urinal filled to the brim.

"Don't come near me or I'll throw this on you and have my uncle, Joe Stalin, beat the shit out of all of you."

A quick turn of the cell door key, and before he could react, we were all in the cell and he was subdued. The doctor injected him with a fast-acting sedative, and in a matter of seconds he was quiet, without a drop of blood or urine being spilled.

Following the explosive escape attempt in May 1946, several inmates became mentally deranged. While most victims were only temporarily affected, one inmate became violent and required special treatment. Johnson was a huge, strong man assigned to the garbage crew. He had worked for several years on the garbage detail, hoisting heavy cans and dumping them into the island garbage truck. This work took him into the civilian residential areas and in close contact with the island children. Over the years, this good-natured convict had spoken to many of the island children, giving them coins and marbles he would find as he toured the island. He thoroughly enjoyed his relationship with the youngsters, who knew him and greeted him as he went about his daily routine. The children were in awe of his strength as he tossed heavy garbage cans about as though they were empty boxes. The children loved Johnson and he loved his little friends.

During World War I, he had seen extensive action on the battlefields of France, and suffered traumatic stress syndrome from which he never fully recovered. The gunfire, hand grenades, and other weapons that were used during the 1946 uprising brought back all the hideous memories from his past. Being in a state of confinement during the bombardment magnified his torment.

After order was restored, the garbage crew and a few other outdoor workers resumed their work. But things were not the same as before. Because of the terrorizing gunfire of the previous few days, island youngsters were wary of the convicts, and some were afraid. They scorned their former friend. This preyed on Johnson's already fragile mind, and in a few days, he went completely mad. He beat his head against his cell wall while screaming threats and epithets toward the would-be escapees.

"Let me out of this goddam cell, and give me a machine gun. I'll kill every one of those bloody convict bastards. I'll show them that they can't scare all those little kids. None of my little friends will talk to me anymore; they're all afraid of me. I didn't do anything wrong, but the little kids are scared of me, and they won't talk to me anymore. Let me outta here so I can kill those rotten cons." Several officers were required to bring Johnson to the hospital, where he was placed under restraint. He refused food and soon lost a significant amount of weight. In a relatively short time, his mental and physical condition deteriorated to such an extent that he was transferred to Springfield. It was a tragic situation, and he never recovered.

Inmate suicide attempts were not uncommon. Few were successful because the prisoners were so closely observed. In addition, a number of the attempts were meant to fail, and were staged to get attention or hospitalization. Not all the attempts were ploys, however, and some did result in serious injuries or fatalities.

I had the misfortune of being involved in two suicide attempts, both of which were the real thing. The first occurred when I was working in the west gun gallery, a two-tiered gun cage across the west end of the main cellhouse and D Block. The young officer in D Block at the time was new to prison work, and had only been on the job for a few weeks. It was shaving night in D Block, and one of the convicts used his razor blade to slash his wrists. The officer observed the inmate in the far corner of his cell bleeding profusely from the lacerations and sounded the emergency buzzer. I was at the far end of the gallery using the toilet when the alarm sounded, but got to D Block within seconds. My almost immediate presence on the scene, however, did not mollify the panic of the frantic young officer. As I entered D Block he shouted in horror, "For Christ's sake, Lageson, hurry the hell up. I've got a guy bleeding to death down here." It was an emergency, but clearly not a panic.

I raced to the electric panel board and unlocked the injured man's cell door. In the meantime other officers had arrived to assist the D Block officer. Two officers entered the cell and applied pressure to the wounds to arrest the blood flow, receiving no resistance from the bleeding victim. Tourniquets were applied, and he was taken to the hospital for medical care and psychiatric evaluation. In time he was returned to general population, but made other attempts to injure himself. His next effort at self-destruction involved bashing his head against the wall of his cell. This got him assigned to a padded-wall hospital cell and, ultimately, a transfer to Springfield.

The second case paralleled the first, but this time I was the officer in isolation, and again it was shave night. The inmate involved occupied the end cell on the third tier, so he was the first man to receive his blade, and his was the first blade collected. After handing out all the blades I sat at my desk for a short time, giving the men an opportunity to conclude their shaves before I collected the blades. The prisoners were required to set their blades on the cross bars of their cell doors after they had shaved. At the first cell there was no blade, and the occupant was in his bunk with the blankets pulled up to his neck with his eyes closed.

"Hey, fella," I shouted loudly, "where's your blade?" thinking he was asleep. There was no response, and looking carefully into the cell I could see blood on the sheet hanging below the gray blankets. The inmate looked pale and wasn't moving. Realizing I had a suicide attempt on my hands, I shouted to the officer in the gun gallery to inform all the officers in the main cellhouse of a possible suicide in D Block and raced down the stairs to telephone the hospital and the administrative offices.

While outwardly I was calm and did all the right things, internally, I was in a state of panic. I'd only been on the job for seven months, and suddenly I was confronted with a potential fatality. Although I had been trained for such a situation, now it was really happening. As a custodial officer, I felt responsible for the men under my supervision. Now one of my charges was in danger of dying, and I could not permit that to happen.

Several officers arrived almost immediately and one of them entered the cell with me. We threw back the blankets and found the convict had slashed both wrists. The cut on the right wrist was into an artery, and arterial blood was literally spraying from the wound with every beat of his heart. The left wrist was bleeding significantly, but nothing like the right. Both ankles had been cut and were bleeding. He was lying in a deep pool of blood, seeming unconscious, and appeared to be in serious condition.

Despite his condition, when I applied pressure to stop the bleeding, the convict began to thrash about, splattering blood on everyone and everything in or near the cell. My fellow officer, a husky man in excess of two hundred pounds, sat on the man's feet while I sat on his chest. By so doing we were able to subdue him and stem the blood flow until the medical attendant arrived. The officer assisting me was a multi-year veteran of prison work and totally cool under fire. Both of us were covered with blood by the time it was over, and presented a ghastly sight. After we finished wrapping his wounds, he was taken to the hospital; we knew that, while he was in serious condition, the man would survive. The old timer, realizing I was somewhat shaken, smiled at me and counseled, "Relax, Ernie. After all, he's only a convict." In the hospital, the man was sutured, bandaged, and observed closely for several days. In a few weeks, he was hale and hearty and back in the D Block routine.

The inmate involved had an incredible history of violent conduct, which was why he was in isolation. While at times he appeared completely normal and deported himself well, at other times he committed violent assaults on fellow prisoners. He was transferred to Alcatraz because of his record of violence, and during my tenure on the island, he committed three ferocious attacks on other inmates. Once he stabbed another inmate with a homemade knife as the men were filing into the mess hall. Of course, there were no eyewitnesses among the dozens of men who saw the attack so he was not charged with attempted murder. He did lose 1,500 days of good time and was sent to isolation. On another occasion he gouged a fellow inmate with the broken top of a medicine bottle. Again, there were no witnesses. Finally he stabbed and killed an inmate, for which he was tried and convicted. He received an additional fifteen years for that crime.

On the day of his suicide attempt, I had spent a considerable period of time talking to him about the knife attack with which he had been charged. He vociferously denied the charge, and presented a rational explanation of how he had been wrongfully accused. Regardless of the truth of his argument, his logic, demeanor, and rationality negated any thought that he was suicidal. Yet, only hours later, he would have died had we not violently saved his life. To add to the complexity of the situation, the inmate who was assigned to clean up the cell found a garotte fashioned from the wire at the top of the inmate's whiskbroom. It was a highly effective killing tool. Who was it for? Another inmate? An officer? He had never attacked an officer, but there was always a first time. It was convicts like this who made prisons in general and Alcatraz in particular incredibly dangerous places to live and work.

I was temporarily relieved after the incident to go to our apartment and clean up, for I had literally taken a bloodbath. I was covered with blood from head to foot, and needed a shower and complete change of clothing. At the time my aged mother was visiting us from her home in North Dakota. She had difficulty accepting the fact that her son was living on the island prison, and the sight of me that evening put her into a temporary state of shock.

One of the most interesting psychotics with whom I dealt in D Block was Henri Young. He had a history of suicide attempts, and as a result occupied one of the bottom tier cells near the isolation officer's desk. One shave night, after I had distributed razors to the upper tiers, I delivered one of the specially sealed razors to Young. As he took the razor and other shaving equipment he inquired, "Boss, when are they going to quit giving me this sealed-up razor? They treat me like a psycho."

"Henri," I answered, "as long as you do such things as slash your wrists, you're going to be using this kind of razor. How can you be regarded as anything but a psycho when you do stuff like that?"

"Oh, Mr. Lageson, that stuff's all over. I'd never do anything like that again."

"Why did you do it in the first place?" I asked.

"Well, that's a long story, and when we have more time I'll fill you in on the whole thing."

Young was correct; it was a very long story. Born and raised in Kansas City, Missouri, he was the product of a violent and broken home. There was constant fighting between the parents, who divorced when Henri was fourteen. Following the divorce, his mother remarried, but Henri never got along with his stepfather, and soon left home for good. He had no trade or employment, and was basically a wanderer. One of the few things he learned from his father was how to steal, and by the time he was twenty-one, he was serving time in the Montana State Penitentiary for robbery and burglary. Four months after his release, he was again in prison, this time the Washington State Penitentiary, serving a ten-year sentence for burglary. While seeking parole, Young spent considerable time planning a bank robbery. Upon release, he committed three felonies within three weeks, all with the use of firearms. That crime spree landed him in the federal penitentiary at McNeil Island, Washington. Because of numerous prison infractions and his violent nature, he was transferred to Alcatraz after only five months at McNeil. Young's Alcatraz file documented more than thirty-five instances of misconduct while on The Rock, including attempted escape, destruction of property, sabotage, rioting, participation in a strike, encouraging other inmates to attack officers, assault, and murder.

His career of misconduct at Alcatraz reached its pinnacle in December 1940, when he stalked and killed Rufus McCain, an inmate with whom he had attempted to escape two years earlier. This was his second attempt to kill McCain and this time, he was successful. He was tried for murder in the federal court in San Francisco and his lawyers defended the case on the theory that Young was insane. It was argued that he had been driven insane by the various periods of solitary confinement and isolation to which he had been subjected as punishment during the preceding three years. Although it was a clear case of first-degree murder and the United States attorney who tried the case was seeking the death penalty, good lawyering by Young's defense counsel managed to convince the jury that Young, not McCain, was the victim and Alcatraz rather than Young was the aggressor. He was convicted of involuntary manslaughter and given a three-year sentence.

While a victory in court, it was the end of Young's days in general population, and he spent the next eight years in isolation. During this time he read extensively, studying psychology and psychiatry. He claimed he had cured his mental illness by study and self-treatment. He fancied himself a self-trained psychiatrist, and made himself available to treat fellow convicts who claimed to be insane.

Following the sensational prison break attempt in 1946, the three surviving would-be escapees were tried for murder in the federal court in San Francisco. One of the defendants in that case, Sam Shockley, was defended on the theory of insanity, and Young was called as an expert witness to testify as to Shockley's mental condition. The court did not permit Young to testify as an expert, but he was permitted to give lay testimony of his observations of Shockley's sanity.

While he continued to profess sanity, Young's actions suggested otherwise, and because of his long and violent record, Alcatraz authorities never trusted him back in general population. In 1948, he was transferred to Springfield; his mental condition had deteriorated to the point that he needed more specialized care than he could receive at Alcatraz. At Springfield, he was diagnosed as paranoid schizophrenic, and he remained under close observation and psychiatric care until he completed his sentence in 1954. At that time he was released into the custody of Washington state authorities to begin serving a life sentence for a murder committed many years earlier. Young was paroled in 1972. Soon thereafter, he violated his parole by failing to report to his parole officer. Despite comprehensive searches, Henri Young disappeared, and has never been seen or heard of since.

In 1994, a movie version of the Henri Young murder trial, *Murder In the First*, was released. While it purported to be a true story of Young's background and the trial, it was a complete revision of history. It was also totally in conflict with the autobiographical writings of Young in his file. Despite Hollywood's attempt to portray him otherwise, Young was a vicious, psychotic criminal and the killer of at least two human beings. He can certainly be numbered among the most dangerous men to do time at Alcatraz.

(Left) Henri Young, one of Alcatraz's psychotic killers, who murdered both in and out of prison. A violent killer with suicidal tendencies, he was one of The Rock's most troublesome inmates.

(Right) Rufus McCain, friend and victim of Henri Young. They attempted to escape together in 1939, and Young murdered him in 1940, his second attempt to kill McCain.

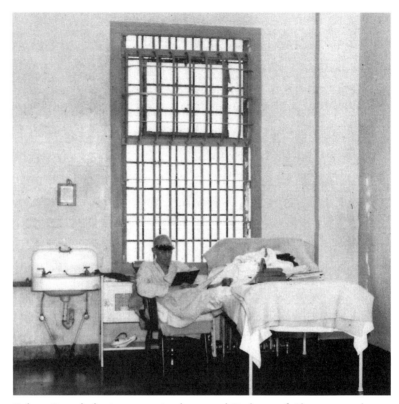

Robert Stroud, the inappropriately named Birdman of Alcatraz, in his hospital cell. Stroud spent seventeen years on Alcatraz, six in isolation and eleven in a hospital cell, where he was isolated from other inmates.

Hospital cells

Chapter XI

Violence in Prison

Prisons are violent places that house violent men. Alcatraz was no exception. During the island's twenty-nine year history as a federal prison, eight prisoners were murdered by fellow prisoners and five committed suicide. Thirteen convicts were either killed by gunfire, drowned, or are believed to have drowned in escape attempts. Two were executed after being found guilty of murder. In addition to their total disregard for the rights and property of others, most of the convicts had relied on violence to accomplish their goals and solve their problems when they lived in the free world. Nothing changed when they went to prison. Locking these individuals in steel and concrete cages did not change their malevolent tendencies, but in many instances, served to stimulate violent conduct, since this was often necessary to stay alive in prison.

Violence could, and did, erupt anywhere in the prison, but the recreation yard was a common site of inmate brutality. Although violence there rarely grew out of the organized competitive activities, the yard was the scene of more violence than any other single venue on the island. Despite the presence of officers on patrol in the yard and heavily armed officers on the yard wall and nearby road tower overlooking the yard, fights and physical attacks regularly took place there. Here were large numbers of unrestrained prisoners supervised by a mere handful of officers. It was the perfect place to settle a grudge. To be effective, the attack had to be swift and deadly, because it would be short-lived, and the assailant would be immediately dispatched to the Hole.

One of the frequently heard expressions was that a man was "doing his own time." This described a prisoner who tried to follow the rules, stay out of trouble, and avoid hostile or negative conduct with other convicts. While many prisoners sought to do their own time, it was often difficult to accomplish, because frequently trouble came that the inmate could not avoid. In the free world, one could avoid a troublemaker and walk away from violence. In prison, the nonviolent inmate had nowhere to go to avoid violence. And trouble could come to a prisoner who had done nothing to deserve it. Another convict might just not like your looks regardless of what you did. Running from trouble could be worse than standing up to it. To be branded a coward would not only be a devastating loss of face and reputation, but would probably bring insults and attacks. In many cases there was no way the nonviolent prisoner could win.

I witnessed several such situations, but one incident in particular stands out. A young inmate assigned to the kitchen detail had, for some reason, become the target of abuse at the hands of a fellow prisoner. He had done nothing to deserve the mistreatment, and avoided trouble to the extent he could. He was slight of build, and clearly had no heart for a fight. The aggressive convict was a highly regarded fighter who could easily cut the young lad down in short order. But in order to maintain his status as a "regular guy" and enjoy the respect of the other inmates, the harassed prisoner regularly joined his fellow kitchen workers in the recreation yard during free time rather than retreat to the safety of his cell. In time, the abusive conduct became too much for him and he lashed back verbally at his tormentor. This was what the bully wanted, and the battle was on. Not unexpectedly, the victim lasted but a few blows, and he received a sound beating before the yard officers could separate the two. But that settled the matter. He had stood up to the heckler, and even though he lost the fight he gained the respect of the other convicts, including the bully. Unfortunately, not all altercations had so satisfactory an outcome.

Another incident occurred in the kitchen, and was mentioned in Chapter X. It was the kitchen worker who had the misfortune to witness two fellow inmates engaged in a sexual act. Whether enraged at being found out or angered by the innocent observer's comments, both men attacked the luckless witness. He was stabbed and cut badly about the head and neck, and given a merciless beating. He was rushed to the hospital where he received the needed medical care; within a few months he was a psychiatric patient and was transferred to Springfield. What role that terrible beating played in his mental deterioration is unknown, but it had to have been a factor. Many men withstood the terrible violence of prison with no apparent harmful after-affects. Others weren't as fortunate, and suffered emotional, neurotic, or psychotic reactions, occasionally with catastrophic results. Here was a convict who was doing his own time, but became involved in an outbreak of violence by simply being in the wrong place at the wrong time. In his case, the results were devastating.

A violent quarrel, leading to murder, occurred less than a month after I had been sworn in as a custodial officer. As was so often the case, the origin of the violence was a prison love affair gone awry. The two inmates had a homosexual relationship, and one of the pair had "cheated" on the other. Rejection fostered hatred, which turned violent. The final act of the drama occurred in the barbershop, when one inmate disemboweled the other with a prison-fashioned knife. The victim died before medical aid arrived. None of the many bystanders had seen anything, and the attacker successfully put forth a plea of self-defense, although he lost significant amounts of statutory good time.

Another violent death occurred in the barbershop a short time later. The lethal weapon that time was the stand upon which the barber's clippers were hung, and the victim received a horrible bludgeoning. Once again, the attacker was acquitted even though an inmate did testify that the defendant was the killer. Six other eyewitnesses testified they had not seen the crime, and the jury disbelieved the one government witness. The killer, in a manner of speaking, "went free." He returned to Alcatraz, was placed in isolation, and lost thousands of days of good time. The inmate who testified for the prosecution had to be transferred to another institution for his own safety.

Although the administration worked diligently to maintain good race relationships, negative incidents could not totally be avoided. While there were occasional episodes of racial violence, most were minor one-on-one incidents. I remember only one major event, and it occurred in the crowded recreation yard on a Sunday afternoon.

Four white convicts were playing a game of handball doubles on the court adjacent to the horseshoe pits when two black inmates asked if they could have the court at the conclusion of the game then in progress. The white players agreed to relinquish the court when their game was over. They had no intention of relinquishing the court, at least not to the black men, and continued their game unreasonably long. It soon became apparent to the black convicts that they were deliberately being kept away from the court by the white men. One of the blacks picked up a horseshoe, the other grabbed one of the shovels used to smooth the sand in the horseshoe pit, and they both advanced toward the white convicts. The prisoners in the area saw the brawl coming, and some moved a safe distance away while others edged in closer to take part in what was about to happen. Suddenly, the melee broke out in full fury, involving fists, feet, horseshoes, shovels, and softball bats, as well as other weapons, which seemed to come out of nowhere. It was a spontaneous eruption that immediately assumed near-riot proportions, although less than half the prisoners in the yard were involved. By the time the yard duty officers could intervene, the battle had become one-sided, with the white convicts gaining superiority over the greatly outnumbered blacks.

The Sunday chapel services ended just as the battle began, and the "parishioners" entered the yard at the height of the fracas. One of the churchgoers was a burly black man who was always ready for a fight with any man, black or white. Seeing what was going on, he ran down the long flight of stairs and into the fray, all the while shouting:

"Equality! Equality! We want equality!"

As he arrived at the center of the action, he was felled by a series of blows to his head by a horseshoe-wielding adversary. He was beaten unconscious, and required hospitalization.

Calm heads among the noninvolved inmates and forceful intervention by the officers soon brought the struggle under control. Once order was restored, the injured men were treated, and the recreation period continued almost as though nothing had happened. Because of the spontaneity of the violence and the impossibility of establishing fault, no disciplinary action was taken. It was yet another example of what so often happened on Alcatraz. Acts of incredible violence would occur.

Severe injuries might result. If identified, the aggressor, and sometimes the aggressive victim, would be disciplined in-house, and the matter would be closed. Acts of savage violence, which would have been punishable by prison terms if committed on the outside, were often dealt with on Alcatraz by loss of good time, and a stretch in the Hole. It was a violent place and the administration knew how to deal with violence.

One of the shortest Alcatraz fights I witnessed took place following the noon meal as the work lines were forming in the yard. Two inmates got into a fight, but because both men were short, the officers in the yard did not see the trouble. The officer in the main tower on the roof of the cellhouse, however, saw the fight immediately, and fired two shots in the air. The shocked fighters thought they were under attack, and ran for cover. The fight was over literally the moment it started, and the two belligerents were hustled off to the Hole.

Fights occasionally occurred in the mess hall or while the prisoners were passing to and from meals. These were generally abortive affairs, because several officers were always on hand to intervene. Inmates and officers alike believed that most such altercations were intended to be short lived. As one convict observer said to me, "Boss, those guys don't want to fight. They're only 'signifying.' If they really wanted to do the job, they'd do it when there weren't so many screws around. What the guards really ought to do is let them finish it."

While a number of the officers may have secretly shared this view, convict altercations were always quickly broken up and the participants separated and confined. This was particularly true when large numbers of prisoners were present. The risk of mass violence always existed, since during such times, the officers were significantly outnumbered. The inmates could not be trusted, and if mob hysteria developed when they were out of their cells, the result could be disastrous.

Officers were rarely attacked during normal prison routine, although such attacks did occur during escape attempts. An attack on an officer would be met with a violently forceful response as well as the loss of statutory good time, and the prisoners knew it. On occasion, however, it did occur, but with dire consequences for the attacker. One such instance took place as the inmates were passing to the yard for recreation one Sunday morning. The attacking inmate had opened one of the drawers of the cell house officer's desk, presumably to get a handball, and the cell house officer reprimanded him condescendingly.

"Listen, boy, don't you ever open the drawers to that desk. No inmate has any business meddling with anything in that desk. If you want anything, you ask for it."

With that, the prisoner flew into a rage and struck out at the officer. The inmate was a huge, powerful man, but almost before he could land a blow, the other officers in the area leapt to the defense of their fellow guard. The prisoner was hammered by two or three officers wielding billy clubs and blackjacks. Before he fully realized what was happening, the convict was in need of medical care. He was quickly rendered unconscious and hauled off to the hospital, where several stitches were required to put his head back together. During the subsequent investigation, he was asked, "What did you think you were going to gain by attacking the officer?"

His answer indicated that he still retained his sense of humor. "Boss, I thought the joint was going soft, but I guess I was wrong."

The inmate involved was a troublesome, unruly prisoner, always in conflict with his fellow prisoners and prison officials. After a short stay in the Hole, then a few weeks in isolation, he was assigned to a work area shop and became a model prisoner. He was courteous to officers and inmates alike, hardworking, and a power for good among the rest of the inmates in his shop.

Force was often necessary to quell inmate violence. Personally, I didn't like to have to use force, and was very much opposed to its excessive use. But there were occasions when those of us in authority had no choice but to appeal to the only level of conduct some convicts would react to, force and pain. Sometimes, as in the case above, it worked. Sometimes it didn't. Sometimes nothing worked.

Chapter XII

The Boys Want to Go Home

The principal responsibility of the warden of a penitentiary is to maintain custody of those men committed to his institution. Preventing escape becomes the paramount function of the institution, from the warden to the newest officer. One of the first lectures we received during our training concerned custody and how it superseded all else. Later, during a personal interview with the warden, this responsibility was reiterated.

The Alcatraz officer was also well aware of the risks he assumed by accepting employment on The Rock. While most of the Alcatraz prisoners did their time with a view to transfer and ultimate parole, the island prison had more than its share of "cons with rabbit blood in their veins." No matter how secure the facility might be, there was always a cunning convict who could find a hole in the security system through which he could run. If a custodial officer stood between the would-be escapee and freedom, the officer's life was at risk. It was a fact of life on Alcatraz with which we all lived.

During the twenty-nine years Alcatraz functioned as a federal prison, thirty-four inmates took part in fourteen escape attempts. Two of those men, Joseph Cretzer and Sam Shockley, tried it twice. The facts of the various attempts included the bloody, the sensational, the foolish, the spontaneous, the well-prepared, and even the humorous. The toll in loss of life and injuries was great. Eight of the fourteen attempted breakouts resulted in fatalities. Eight prisoners and three officers died of injuries received during escape tries. It is assumed that five unaccounted-for inmates also died. Three inmates and fifteen officers were wounded. Two inmates were executed following their conviction for a murder committed during an attempted escape.

Joseph Bowers—1936

Joseph Bowers, the first inmate to attempt escape. He was killed on April 27, 1936, as he scaled the fence surrounding his work area.

The Rock experienced its first attempted breakout on April 27, 1936. The official Alcatraz files describe the event as an unsuccessful escape attempt by Joseph Bowers. However, many of the inmates on the island and Alcatraz critics at the time argued that Bowers was not attempting to escape, but was committing suicide. Whatever his motive, the event cost Bowers his life.

As was the case with many of the Alcatraz prisoners, life did not treat Bowers well. He was born in 1897 to circus performer parents who abandoned him shortly thereafter. He traveled with the circus until he was thirteen. He received no formal education, but during his upbringing, managed to learn to read and write and was allegedly proficient in several languages. At age thirteen he left circus life, and went to sea in the merchant marine. He traveled the world, and was married in Russia in 1919. The marriage ended in divorce the same year.

He was first imprisoned in Oregon in 1928 for auto theft. He later robbed a store containing a small post office, which resulted in his imprisonment in the federal prison at McNeil Island, Washington. He was one of the early prisoners to be sent to Alcatraz, arriving on The Rock in 1934. In his Alcatraz file, he was described as a powerful man of limited mental capacity with an extremely ugly disposition. He was a custodial problem from the outset. Because of his limited employment capabilities, he was assigned to burn trash in a fenced incinerator area on the western side of the island. There he worked under the observation of the nearby road tower officer, and apparently his performance was satisfactory.

On the day of the escape attempt, Road Tower Officer E. F. Chandler observed that Bowers had climbed to the top of the wire fence surrounding the incinerator area. Chandler called to him a couple of times to come down from the fence, but the commands were ignored. Chandler fired two warning shots over the inmate's head, and the gunfire was also disregarded. When Bowers climbed over the fence and began descending on the other side Chandler fired at him. Chandler aimed at the prisoner's legs, but one of the bullets struck him in the chest penetrating his right lung. He clung to the outside of the fence for a brief time, then plunged to his death on the rocks seventy-five feet below.

Following the incident, the suggestion was made that he had climbed the fence to feed the gulls, or that he was attempting to retrieve pieces of paper that had blown to the top of the fence, and the officer had shot him in cold blood. Another theory suggested that Bowers committed suicide to escape the brutal conditions on Alcatraz. Knowing he would be shot, he intentionally provoked the officer to kill him. The suicide theory was bolstered by the fact that a year or so earlier Bowers had attempted to cut his throat with a piece of broken glass. The investigation that followed, however, established that Bowers was climbing over the fence and died as a result of an escape attempt.

Ralph Roe – Theodore Cole—1937

Ralph Roe and Theodore Cole slipped away from the mat shop on a foggy day in December, 1937, and attempted to swim to freedom. Both men disappeared, never to be heard of again.

The first convicts to make it off the island in an escape attempt were Ralph Roe and Theodore Cole in December 1937. The twenty-one-year-old Cole had a violent criminal history dating back to the age of fourteen. A robber, burglar, and murderer, he had served various prison terms during his short life, escaping from some prisons and attempting to escape from others. At one point he was sentenced to death in the electric chair, but his sentence was reduced following pressure from women's groups and civil rights organizations. The death sentence was probably improper since he had only been convicted of armed robbery not associated with a homicide.

While serving time in Leavenworth, Cole met Ralph Roe, and the two became lifelong friends. Roe, like Cole, had a troubled childhood, and was convicted of his first crime at the age of seventeen. He committed numerous armed robberies, many involving violent conduct, and during one shootout, his accomplice was killed. Roe was eventually sentenced by the federal court to ninety-nine years for armed robbery and kidnapping with the recommendation that he be sent to Alcatraz. Both prisoners came in the same shipment of convicts from Leavenworth to Alcatraz in October 1935.

They made their break from the mat shop located on the lower floor of the model shop building. In the mat shop, old automobile tires were cut up and made into rubber deck mats for use on navy and merchant marine ships. It is believed that the two prisoners spent several months planning their escape.

By 1 p.m. on the day of the escape try, the inmates were back at work following the noon meal. The officer who supervised their work also patrolled the nearby blacksmith shop. While he was in the blacksmith shop, Cole and Roe cut the frame and broke out a small window through which they were able to escape to the outside. Scaling the barbed-wire-topped cyclone fence surrounding the work area, they entered the water using two empty five-gallon fuel cans as flotation devices. A dense fog blanketed the bay to such an extent that even normal boat traffic was reduced. At the time of the breakout, the tide was running out to sea at approximately nine miles per hour. After entering the water, the two men were observed for a short time by a number of inmates in the vicinity, then they disappeared into the fog. One of the convict witnesses reported that Roe appeared to struggle trying to stay afloat before he disappeared. No trace of them was ever found, and following an extensive investigation over a lengthy period of time, it was concluded that both men drowned. It is believed that the men became disoriented in the heavy fog, and were carried out to sea by the swift tide.

Rufus "Whitey" Franklin – James Lucas – Thomas Limerick—1938

"Whitey" Franklin, James Lucas, and Thomas Limerick beat officer Royal C. Cline to death during an escape attempt in May 1938. Limerick was killed, Franklin was wounded, and Lucas surrendered.

The first Alcatraz custodial officer to lose his life in the line of duty died in May 1938 when three career criminals attempted a vicious and violent escape. Rufus "Whitey" Franklin began his criminal career at the age of thirteen by stealing an automobile. At sixteen, he was arrested for possession of a loaded pistol, and by age seventeen, had been sentenced to life in prison for first degree murder. He was granted a temporary parole while in prison to attend his mother's funeral. He took the opportunity to rob a bank in Cedar Bluff, Alabama, which earned him a trip to Alcatraz in the summer of 1936.

James Lucas also had a violent criminal history, and was serving thirty years for bank robbery, attempted murder, and escape. Prison did not curb Lucas's violent tendencies, and in June 1936, he attempted to kill Al Capone with a weapon made of a single scissors blade.

Thomas Limerick had a long criminal record that included armed robbery, burglary, auto theft, and escape. Following a violent bank robbery in Dell Rapids, South Dakota, the sawed-off shotgun-wielding Limerick received a life sentence. He was incarcerated in Leavenworth in June 1935, and in October of that year was transferred to Alcatraz.

About two o'clock in the afternoon of April 23, 1938, the three inmates were working in the furniture shop in the model shop building. Arming themselves with a hammer and several pieces of metal, they attacked their supervisor, Officer Royal Cline, who died the next day from his wounds. After beating Officer Cline into unconsciousness, they broke through a fourth-floor window and climbed to the roof. They cut their way through the barbed wire enclosure and attacked Officer Harold Stites in the model shop tower on the roof. Their ultimate plans were not entirely clear, but supposedly they were after Stites's guns.

They attacked the glass-enclosed tower with their primitive weapons, but could not penetrate the shatterproof glass walls. Upon coming under attack, Stites opened fire, killing Limerick and wounding Franklin. While the shatterproof glass withstood the inmates' attack, it was not bulletproof, and Stites was able to fire through it at the convicts. Realizing that further efforts were pointless, Lucas surrendered.

Following a three-week trial in the federal court in San Francisco, both Lucas and Franklin were convicted of first-degree murder, and received life sentences. While the escape attempt had been foiled by the cool conduct of Officer Stites, eight years later, in May 1946, Stites would lose his life during an explosive and bloody escape attempt.

Arthur "Doc" Barker – William Martin – Dale Stamphill
Henri Young – Rufus McCain—1939

Arthur "Doc" Barker   William Martin   Dale Stamphill   Rufus McCain

Arthur "Doc" Barker, William Martin, and Dale Stamphill, along with
Henri Young and Rufus McCain, sawed their way out of D Block in
January 1939. They were all captured on the rocky beach. Barker
later died from wounds he received when he tried to swim away from
the island.

In January 1939, five inmates under the leadership of Arthur "Doc" Barker,
the sole survivor of the notorious Ma Barker Gang, carried out an incredible escape
from the cellhouse in the middle of the night. The inmates sawed their way out of
their D Block cells, then through a cellhouse window before being stopped by a hail
of bullets as they sought to build a driftwood raft on the rocky beach.

In addition to Barker, a notorious robber, killer, and marauder of the 1930s,
the participants included some of Alcatraz's most infamous inmates. Dale Stamphill
was serving life for kidnapping and robbery. William Martin was serving twenty-five
years for armed robbery. Henri Young was a murderer, bank robber, and incorrigible convict serving a twenty-year term. Rufus McCain was doing ninety-nine years
for kidnapping, bank robbery, and escape.

Months earlier, as part of their overall plan, all five convicts had taken active
roles in a work stoppage and strike. As punishment for their conduct, the five were
placed in D Block, which was where they wanted to be. At that time, D Block was

not separately enclosed, but was part of the main cellhouse. In addition, the cells in isolation had not been modernized, but were of the old, non-tool-proof steel installed by the army decades earlier. Over a period of months, the five were able to cut through the soft steel bars of their cells, enabling them to be free in D Block. Using cutting tools and a bar spreader, they were then able to break through the bars on the outside windows, break the glass, and escape from the cellhouse. The ultimate breakout came in the middle of the night when custodial activity was reduced.

After about thirty minutes of freedom, their absence was noted during a routine count, and the escape alarm was sounded. An armed posse soon located the convicts on the beach, and charged the group. When Stamphill and Barker ignored orders to surrender and ran into the water, they were brought down in a blaze of gunfire. Barker's wounds proved to be fatal, and he died the following morning. Stamphill recovered, and along with the other three survivors, served terms in solitary and isolation.

After two years in isolation, the four surviving inmates returned to general population. Apparently Young blamed McCain for the failure of the escape attempt, and developed a deep hatred for his fellow conspirator. Once back in general population, Young stalked and stabbed McCain to death with two hand-fashioned knives. In time, the site of the capture became known as Barker Beach and that name persists to the present.

Joseph Cretzer – Sam Shockley – Arnold Kyle – Lloyd Barkdoll—1941

Joseph Cretzer   Sam Shockley   Arnold Kyle   Lloyd Barkdoll

Joseph Cretzer, Sam Shockley, Arnold Kyle , and Lloyd Barkdoll
tried unsuccessfully to break out of the mat shop in May 1941.
Cretzer and Shockley would participate in a second escape
attempt in 1946.

On May 21, 1941, Joseph Cretzer and Sam Shockley would make their first of two escape attempts from Alcatraz. Also involved in that breakout was Arnold Kyle, Cretzer's brother-in-law, and Lloyd Barkdoll. All four men were serving lengthy sentences, and at the time were working in the mat shop. It was believed that Barkdoll, organized the breakout attempt. He was a violent and ruthless criminal, serving life for a series of bank robberies in Oregon. Kyle was a career criminal who went to jail for the first time when he was fifteen, and went on to become an accomplished holdup man.

Cretzer and Kyle headed one of the most notorious bank robbery gangs in the nation and terrorized the West Coast banking industry for several years. They committed dozens of robberies, several involving shootouts with bank guards and police. Born in Montana, Cretzer lived for some time in the San Francisco Bay Area. He was the youngest of three sons, all of whom became violent criminals. Both of his brothers were serving lengthy prison terms by the time Joe was arrested for the first time at age fifteen. In time, his criminal career escalated to the point that he became number five on the FBI's list of the ten most wanted criminals in America, an accomplishment in which he took great pride. It also garnered him considerable respect from his fellow Alcatraz inmates.

Cretzer and Kyle met while serving time together at the Preston Reformatory Industrial School in Ione, California. They were discharged at the same time in 1931 and became partners in crime. Eventually, the two men married one another's sisters and made their criminal association a family affair. Their partnership continued until Cretzer's death by gunfire during the sensational escape attempt in May 1946.

Sam Shockley was at once a dangerous convict and a pathetic soul. Born into abject poverty, he left school when he was seven years old to work on the family farm in rural Oklahoma. He had an IQ of 68, and as an adult, had the mental age of an eight- to ten-year-old-child. Shockley left home when he was a teenager, but with no education or skills, there was little he could do to support himself. For several years he got by doing odd jobs and committing petty crimes.

In time, he ended up in the Oklahoma State Reformatory where he suffered a severe beating and head injury at the hands of another inmate. After his release about a year later, he received another serious head injury in a struggle with police officers while resisting arrest. His family claimed that he was never the same after those two beatings.

In 1938, Shockley and an accomplice robbed a small-town bank in Paoli, Oklahoma. As part of their getaway, they kidnapped D.F. Pendley, the bank president, and his wife, the bank cashier. The holdup netted $947.38, the most successful take of Shockley's life. He remained at large for about ten days before being captured at his brother's home. He received a twenty-five-year sentence and was sent to Leavenworth. There he engaged in frequent outbreaks of violence toward the custodial staff and was ultimately transferred to Alcatraz.

Examination and evaluation at Alcatraz established that in addition to retardation, Shockley suffered from schizophrenic paranoia. He was a prime candidate for the psychiatric ward at the medical facility at Springfield, but his case somehow fell between the cracks, and he remained at Alcatraz. He could not hold a job, and was constantly in trouble. Known as "Crazy Sam" to convicts and officers alike, he hallucinated, heard voices coming out of the walls of his cell and his toilet, and was a highly difficult inmate to control. He served several periods in isolation for repeated violations of prison regulations. His IQ actually fell over the years from 68 to 54, an indication that he was regressing mentally. His paranoia deepened. He constantly complained that the prison administration was trying to poison him and was beaming harmful rays at him through the light fixture in his cell.

The escape attempt began just after the prisoners returned to work following the noon meal when they overpowered their supervising officer, Clyne Stoops. After tying and gagging Stoops, they began prying out and cutting through a steel-framed window. After about thirty minutes, another officer entered the shop on routine patrol and was captured. A short time later, a third officer entered the shop and was also captured. The window frame and its tool-proof bars proved to be an impossible hurdle, and as the prisoners struggled with the window, Captain Paul Madigan entered the shop. Madigan was initially overpowered by the inmates, but succeeded in convincing them that their escape attempt had failed. Satisfied they could not cut through the window, the prisoners gave up their effort, freed Madigan and the other officers, and accepted their lengthy punishment, first in solitary then in isolation.

John Bayless—1941

John Bayless made a spontaneous dash for freedom on a foggy day in September 1941, and was captured almost immediately.

On September 15, 1941, John Bayless, a Midwestern bank robber serving fifty years, made a wild, unplanned attempt to escape, which was an instant failure. He was working on the garbage crew, and it was near the end of the workday. In the relaxed, end-of-the-day routine, he made a sudden break for freedom under the cover of a heavy afternoon fog. Minutes after he slipped away, the officer in charge of the crew became aware of his absence and notified the armory. The escape siren sounded about the same time that Bayless reached the rocky beach. He removed his shirt, shoes, and socks and entered the water, hoping to swim to freedom. He had difficulty staying afloat in the frigid, choppy water of the bay, and was also hampered by injuries he had sustained scrambling over the fence and rocks getting to the water. He was soon spotted by a search party of officers, and quickly apprehended.

After an appropriate period of time in solitary and isolation, Bayless returned to the general population. In time, he became one of the more effective cellhouse lawyers, writing writs for himself and others. The federal district court in San Francisco finally granted him a hearing on a writ of habeas corpus. His writ argued that his conviction was illegal because he had not been properly represented by counsel. At the hearing on his writ, Bayless made another daring dash for freedom. It was judicial policy to remove a prisoner's manacles while he was in court, and Bayless thought his chances warranted a try. He overpowered one of the bailiffs, but this escape effort was even less successful than his first. He was quickly tackled and knocked unconscious by another bailiff.

He was convicted of attempted escape and given an additional five-year sentence. He returned to The Rock, where he maintained a good record, earning a transfer back to Leavenworth in 1950. He was paroled in 1951, but confirmed thief that he was, couldn't stay out of trouble. He robbed a bank in Los Angeles, and as part of his escape, boarded a commercial airline flight to the East Coast. The law was immediately on his trail and he was arrested as he stepped off the plane. Tried and convicted, he arrived back at Alcatraz in August 1952, one of the few prisoners to do multiple terms on the Rock.

James Boarman – Fred Hunter – Harold Brest – Floyd Hamilton—1943

James Boarman   Fred Hunter   Harold Brest   Floyd Hamilton

James Boarman, Fred Hunter, Harold Brest, and Floyd Hamilton
entered the water at the northwest point of the island on the afternoon
of April 13, 1943. Boarman was shot and killed in the water, and the
other three were captured.

On April 13, 1943, the area outside the mat shop at the northwest corner of the island was the scene of another escape attempt. James Boarman, Fred Hunter, Harold Brest, and Floyd Hamilton were constructing the cement blocks used to anchor the heavy steel cable anti-submarine net across the Golden Gate. In addition to the concrete work, some of the servicing and maintenance of the buoys was also carried out in this area.

Boarman was a small-time hoodlum who had been in and out of jail since he was seventeen. Armed robberies and auto theft were his principal crimes, and his prison file indicated that he was a "reckless, unstable psychopath, who was not material for rehabilitation."

Harold Brest went to jail for the first time at the age of fifteen. Over his life of crime, he committed hundreds of robberies throughout Pennsylvania, Ohio, Illinois, Michigan, Wisconsin, and Minnesota. He once admitted that he had committed so may armed robberies that it would be impossible for him to recall them all. He eventually found his way to Alcatraz, where he was serving a life sentence plus two twenty-five-year terms, and one of five years.

Floyd Hamilton was one of the most prominent inmates ever to serve time on Alcatraz. He lived a relatively normal family life as a child, attending Sunday school, doing well in public school, and marrying at the age of nineteen. He worked for a time as a pipe fitter in an oil refinery, but when he lost his job and could not support himself and his wife, he turned to crime. In short order, he was one of the most famous criminals in America as the getaway car driver for the famous Bonnie and Clyde Barrows Gang. In the 1930s, he was considered an instant suspect in nearly every violent crime that occurred in the Dallas, Texas, area. For a time prior to his arrest, he enjoyed the distinction of being ranked number one on the FBI's Ten Most Wanted list. As such, Hamilton was the most wanted criminal in America. This history set him apart as a virtual icon during his incarceration on Alcatraz.

Fred Hunter was a "torpedo" (gunman) for the Barker-Karpis Gang, and was another of the Alcatraz convicts who had made the list of the Ten Most Wanted criminals in America during his criminal career. He was serving twenty-five years for the kidnapping of William A. Hamm, president of the Hamm Brewing Company and Edward G. Bremer, a prominent Minnesota banker.

As D Block officer on the afternoon of April 13, 1943, I was supervising the isolation inmates in the yard. Among my charges were a number of prior attempted escapees including Barkdoll, Cretzer, Kyle, Lucas, and Franklin. The inmates were all engaged in various activities, and there was relative peace among the isolation group. Suddenly, the afternoon calm was shattered by gunfire from the northwest end of the island. Then came the wail of the escape siren.

What should I do? I thought. Here I was surrounded by fifteen of the most desperate prisoners on the island during a prison break. As I scanned the stunned group I could see their eyes bulge and their bodies tense. In the minds of all of them was the same thought; *I hope they make it, and what can I do to help?*

I ordered the inmates to the foot of the cellhouse steps, and told them to remain there until further instructed. Before I did anything else, I looked up at the road tower at the corner of the yard wall. Officer John Barker, on duty in the tower, stood on the walkway of the tower facing away from me and toward the water with his rifle in a firing position. Suddenly he swung around to face the recreation yard and pointed his rifle at my isolation contingent and me. His gesture was totally reassuring.

He later told me, "Ernie, I was going to shoot down at the swimming figures in the water, but when I glanced into the yard and saw the look on Barkdoll's face, I thought I'd better cover you." Standing where the prisoners had a clear view of him, he rammed a cartridge into the chamber of the rifle and pointed the gun directly at the band of D Block convicts standing with me at the bottom of the stairs. Not one of the prisoners moved or said a word. There was no cheering or commenting. They just stood there, frozen in place watching Barker and his loaded rifle. The cellhouse door soon opened and I moved the convicts up the stairs and back to their cells in D Block. Here they anxiously awaited news of the escape attempt while engaged in animated discussion about what was going on outside. Although I gave no indication of interest, I was as curious as they were, and extremely thankful for the presence of John Barker and his loaded Springfield rifle.

The would-be escapees had planned and prepared for months. During their preparation they would individually enter the then-unused Model Shop Building and work at cutting through the bars and window frame on one of the windows on the ground floor. When the window frame had been cut sufficiently to break out the window, the group was ready to go, and simply waited for the right foggy day.

On the day of the escape, there was a thick fog blanketing Alcatraz and San Francisco Bay. The inmates overpowered the two officers supervising the work area, tied them up, and gagged them. Just as they were about to break out, Captain Weinhold entered the building on a routine inspection of the area, and he too was overpowered, tied, and gagged. The men then left the building through the broken window and, with the aid of boards and a tarpaulin scaled the barbed wire-topped cyclone fence and made their way to the water. Hunter fell climbing over the fence, injuring himself sufficiently that he did not feel he could attempt the dangerous swim to freedom. Upon getting to the beach, he hid in one of the caves along the rocky coastline. The others removed their clothes and covered their bodies with heavy industrial grease as protection from the raw cold of the water. They had fashioned crude flotation devices made of rubber, and one of them had an inflatable rubber cushion from the hospital. They also had two tightly sealed one-gallon paint cans containing army uniforms secreted from the dry-cleaning plant. The cans, tied together with twine, served as flotation devices, and the uniforms would be worn once they reached the mainland.

Officer Frank Johnson in the model shop tower atop the Model Shop Building became suspicious when he could not reach the supervising officers below by phone. He contacted the armory to report his concerns, then went out on the roof of the building to inspect the area. As Johnson scanned the bay waters, Weinhold freed himself of his gag and was able to sound his whistle. This further alerted Johnson, who intensified his search of the fog-shrouded water below. He soon sighted the men in the water and opened fire on them. Boarman was shot in the head and died instantly. Brest abandoned his effort to escape and began simply treading water, trying to support Boarman's body. The two were soon sighted by the island motor launch, and Brest was hauled aboard. While officers were trying to lift Boarman's body onto the boat by means of the inmate's belt, the belt broke and the body disappeared under the water. It was never recovered.

Hamilton swam to a small rock about two hundred yards west of the island, known to the island residents as "Little Alcatraz." While holding onto the rock and resting, Hamilton came under extensive gunfire and ducked under the water. He eventually made his way back to Alcatraz and hid in the same cave as Hunter. Hunter was captured within an hour, but the search party didn't find Hamilton.

There was a sharp division of opinion as to Hamilton's fate. Some officers claimed to have seen him go under the water during the escape attempt. Others felt that he was still somewhere in one of the caves hiding under driftwood and other flotsam. The former theory prevailed, and after many hours of unsuccessful search-ing, he was declared dead and the hunt was called off.

On Friday morning, two days later, I was again in the yard with my isolation charges for their second weekly outing. Suddenly, a signal from the yard wall officer directed me to take my recreation detail to the far side of the yard, as there was about to be a movement of inmate personnel through the wall gate. This was not an unusual procedure, so the inmates ambled to one corner of the yard and waited for the gate to open and the traffic to pass through the yard. As we all watched, the gate opened and Captain Weinhold entered the yard escorting a dirty, disheveled, nude, blanket-draped figure. It was Floyd Hamilton, who had previously been declared dead by those investigating the escape attempt.

Weinhold had not been satisfied with the investigation report, and made his own inspection of the abandoned industries building. As he moved about through the the building, he had come upon Hamilton hiding there. The chill water, combined with the injuries he sustained as he crawled out of the window, had been too much for the outlaw. After spending considerable time in the cave, he had crawled back the way he had gone out. During the time he was hiding in the cave, officers had actually walked over him as he lay concealed under heaps of old tire casings and other rubbish. He even repeated portions of the conversation of the search party to prove he had been there. It was yet another example of the invulnerability of Alcatraz. The combination of the rocky cliffs, the cold bay water, and armed men were more than a match for those convicts who would challenge the holding power of The Rock.

Huron "Ted" Walters—1943

Huron "Ted" Walters slipped away from the laundry while working there on a Saturday during reduced security. Injured when he fell climbing over the fence, he simply waited at the water's edge to be captured.

On August 7, 1943, Huron "Ted" Walters, who was serving thirty years for bank robbery and was a criminal partner of Floyd Hamilton on the outside, made a lone wolf attempt to escape. It was a Saturday afternoon, and only the laundry, backlogged with military orders, was working. A crew of inmates had volunteered to work, although they were entitled to the day off. Because it was a Saturday and extra officers were needed in the recreation yard and on cellhouse shakedown duty, only one officer was supervising the laundry. Also, the tower in the work area was not manned.

Taking advantage of this reduced security, Walters was able to sneak out of the laundry. He made his way to a section of the fence that was out of the line of vision of the towers that were manned. He had two one-gallon paint cans with army uniforms sealed inside. Over the months, he had also collected forty-two dollars in cash from the pockets of uniforms, which he intended to use once he got to the mainland. Walters had obtained a pair of electrician's wire cutters to cut through the barbed wire atop the fence, but the tool was too small to cut the wire. He therefore piled some packing crates on top of one another to get over the fence. As he cautiously climbed over the razor sharp wire at the top of the fence, he lost his grip and fell several feet to the ground below. The fall produced disabling pain, which ended his getaway plans. He managed to get to the water, but because of his injury, decided against trying to swim. The laundry officer noted Walter's absence after only a matter of minutes, and notified the armory. Although the alarm did not sound, the island went into escape mode.

Most of the inmates were in the yard enjoying recreational activities as this one-man escape plot was unfolding. I was assigned to the west end of the cellhouse, and my duties included controlling the door to the recreation yard. The quiet of the afternoon was interrupted by a telephone call from the associate warden directing me to bring all prisoners in from the yard and lock them in their cells. He offered no explanation, which was unusual, but I did as ordered, thankful for having the extra officers to help move the inmates from the yard into their cells.

Throwing open the door to the yard, I sounded a few shrill whistle blasts, the signal for the inmates to line up and file back into the cellhouse. Knowing that they were being called in early, there was much complaining among the prisoners. Many of them looked cautiously skyward, suspecting a Japanese air attack.

"Must be an air raid," several of them suggested.

In a few minutes the laundry crew arrived and joined the rest of the convicts heading back to their cells. In short order, the entire general population was back in their cells, and a count was called. As the count was being taken, the escape siren sounded, and so did the inmates. Some screamed for joy, others booed, and they all seemed to be shouting. Numerous calls went out to the unknown escapees: "I hope you guys make it!" Near pandemonium reigned in the cellhouse.

In the meantime, a Coast Guard cutter arrived on the scene and sighted Walters sitting on the rocks on the western shore of the island. About the same time, a group of officers led by Associate Warden Miller and Captain Weinhold moved in and captured Walters without a struggle. Because of his injury, he required hospitalization for more than a week before he did his stint in solitary and later, isolation.

John Giles—1945

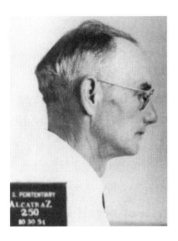

John Giles left the island on July 31, 1945, on the motor vessel *General Frank M. Coxe* posing as an Army telephone repairman. His was one of the most clever and humorous escape attempts in Alcatraz history.

The most elaborate one-man escape try was carried out by a slight, unassuming inmate who worked on the dock. A small-time holdup man, John Giles was serving five to ten years for robbery when he was pardoned in 1918 by authorities in the state of Washington, based on his promise to enlist in the army. Instead of enlisting, he returned to his former career as an armed robber and killed a deputy sheriff in a shoot-out following a robbery in Oregon. He was convicted of murder and given a life sentence. After sixteen uneventful years in state prison, he escaped, and while a fugitive, took part in a mail train robbery in Salt Lake City. Following his arrest and conviction, Giles was sentenced to another twenty-five years and sent to McNeil Island. Because of his escape history, he was transferred to Alcatraz in 1935.

At Alcatraz, Giles was a model prisoner. When I met him in 1942, he was fifty years old, a slim, almost emaciated-appearing individual. He was quiet and spoke very little to either inmates or officers. Giles was well-read and could discuss several subjects with considerable authority. Because of his age and lack of physical strength, he was usually given less strenuous jobs, such as sweeping and tidying up. Giles was often assigned to my custody for special assignments since I got along well with him. Periodically, on Sunday afternoons, Giles and I would patrol the beach at low tide with an axe, chopping up and burning driftwood. It was a security measure to eliminate wood that could be use to construct a raft for an escape attempt. During these forays Giles would expound on an array of subjects ranging from Bay Area tide pool life to national politics. He had once been a writer of short stories, a number of which had been published in the pulp magazines of the day, and we would also discuss literary subjects.

Once a week, Giles and I would tour Building 64, one of the island apartment houses, sweeping the floors and tidying up in general. He enjoyed those special assignments, for they broke the otherwise monotonous inmate life and gave him a chance to discuss subjects with me that were beyond the intellect of most of his contemporaries. During his many years working on the dock, Giles had ample opportunity to study the routine of the dock and the details of both the island and army boat operations.

The *General Frank M. Coxe* was a large harbor boat operated by the army between Pier Four on the mainland and Fort McDowell on Angel Island. As a courtesy to the Alcatraz residents, the army boat made several stops each day at Alcatraz going to and coming from the mainland. Whenever a boat came alongside the Alcatraz pier, the inmate dock workers moved to the far side of the dock away from the vessel and remained there until the boat departed. It was a standard procedure, taken for granted by officers and inmates alike, and unfortunately, it became a routine.

Over time, Giles managed to collect an entire army uniform from the dry cleaning that came to the island. He hid the clothing under the dock until he was ready to make his move. On the day in question, the *Coxe* arrived at Alcatraz from the mainland on its way to Angel Island. While the boat was unloading passengers, Giles slipped into his army uniform and scrambled along the pilings under the dock. He stepped from the underside of the dock onto the boat wearing the uniform of an army sergeant. When he came aboard, he was observed by a real sergeant in the Military Police, whose job it was to check for unauthorized personnel. Given the fact that the nation was at war and Fort McDowell was a military installation, the MP was on the lookout for spies, not escaping convicts. Giles was carrying tools and a flashlight, and explained to the MP that he was an electrician doing work on the telephone cables on the island. The soldier was not convinced and reported the incident to the captain of the *Coxe*. Giles immediately headed for a men's rest room, where he waited until the boat left Alcatraz.

As soon as the boat left, a count was taken and Giles' absence was noted. A call immediately went to Angel Island advising of the situation and requesting that no one be allowed off the boat until a detail of Alcatraz custodial officers was there. The island motor launch, with the associate warden, captain, and several officers aboard, left immediately and was docked before the *Coxe* arrived at Angel Island. When the passengers were allowed to leave the *Coxe*, Giles walked down the gangway into the hands of half-dozen officers. He was quickly whisked back to Alcatraz, stripped of his military clothing, and placed in solitary confinement.

I didn't see Giles again until after he had done his time in solitary and later isolation. He was back in general population, but no longer working on the dock. Since I knew him so well, I felt comfortable kidding him about the event, which by then had made him a celebrity among the convicts. "So, Jack, it looks like you've been demoted. The last time I saw you, you were a sergeant. What happened?"

"Yeah, Boss, they lowered the boom on me. It'll be another ten years before I can get promoted to sergeant again."

When Giles was tried in federal court for attempted escape, his attorney raised a novel defense. He argued that the indictment under which Giles was being charged was faulty. He claimed his client was charged with attempted escape when in reality Giles had actually escaped, since he was completely beyond the physical restraint and safekeeping of his custodians. Clever though it was, it did not impress the court and Giles got another five years to go with his already lengthy sentence. He remained in general population for several years and was eventually transferred to Leavenworth. He was paroled several years later and lived a crime-free life until his death at the age of eighty-four.

Floyd P. Wilson—1956

Wilson slipped away from the dock one afternoon and remained at large for over eleven hours. He was captured on the beach without ever leaving the island.

Another unsuccessful one-man runaway attempt took place on July 23, 1956. This time, it was forty-one-year-old Floyd P. Wilson, serving life for murder, a crime committed on what was his first criminal effort. Wilson was an unemployed carpenter trying to support a wife and five children during a particularly frigid Maryland winter. He set out to steal enough money to buy a ton of coal to heat his house. At the time, coal sold for less than twenty dollars a ton. He held up a young supermarket employee on his way to deposit the day's cash receipts, an amount in excess of $10,000. When the messenger resisted, Wilson shot and killed the young man. Wilson's death sentence was commuted to life in prison by then President Harry Truman. When he was suspected of planning an escape from the federal penitentiary at Atlanta, Wilson was transferred to Alcatraz.

On Alcatraz, Wilson was a loaner, rarely mingling with his fellow prisoners. He had a poor work record and was periodically placed on report for minor rule infractions. He rarely took advantage of the recreation yard, preferring to spend his free time reading in his cell. In time, he was assigned to the dock, where he seemed to get along reasonably well.

His escape plan was a simple one: sneak away from the dock, hide until it was dark, then make a raft of driftwood and float to freedom. Like all prior similar efforts, Wilson's plan failed.

Wilson somehow obtained a lengthy piece of rope, which he hid somewhere on the dock. During a quiet moment, he slipped away from the dock and made his way to the rocky beach. He had only a ten-minute head start on his pursuers, having been present at 3:40 p.m. but missing at the 3:50 p.m. count. He hid among the large rocks at the water's edge until it was dark, and, despite the efforts of dozens of custodial officers, he was not found. Throughout the night, the Alcatraz motor launch, Coast Guard vessels, and the San Francisco police boat circled the island without locating the missing convict. About 3:00 a.m., Wilson was spotted hiding in a depression in one of the boulders near the waterline. He still had the rope with which he had planned to build a raft. Free for more than eleven hours, his efforts gained him nothing more than a stretch in solitary, followed by a lengthier sentence in isolation. He was transferred to Atlanta when Alcatraz closed in 1963, and was paroled in 1971. Wilson lived a crime-free life until his death in 1974.

Aaron Burgett – Clyde Johnson—1958

Aaron Burgett

Clyde Johnson

Aaron Burgett and Clyde Johnson attempted to swim to freedom on a foggy day in September 1958. Johnson, overcome by the frigid, choppy bay waters, immediately returned. Burgett was not found, prompting an extensive search and the issuance of a national all-points bulletin. Two weeks later, Burgett's body was found floating only a few hundred feet from where he entered the water.

Aaron Burgett and Clyde Johnson picked a foggy day in September 1958 to attempt their escape. Burgett was serving twenty-six years for post office robbery, and Clyde Johnson was doing forty years for bank robbery. Both men had violent backgrounds involving assaults with firearms and were considered escape threats prior to their transfer to Alcatraz. Johnson had enjoyed his status as Public Enemy # Two prior to his conviction in 1949. At Alcatraz, both men established good records, and were assigned to the garbage detail. Officer Harold Miller, a relatively new officer on Alcatraz, had just been assigned as officer in charge of the garbage detail and was still learning the job. The escape attempt was well-planned, and it was obvious that the prisoners had worked on the details of the breakout for several months.

Among the duties of the garbage crew was to clean the pathway that led down to the water's edge below the civilian housing area. While working in that area and out of the view of any guard towers, the inmates overpowered Officer Miller and tied him to a eucalyptus tree behind a large wooden warning sign after gagging him and taping his eyes shut. They then made their way to the southwest corner of the island, where they entered the water. The pair greased their bodies to protect themselves from the approximately fifty-degree water. They had fashioned crude facemasks and snorkels as well as wooden fins, which they attached to their feet. Burgett entered the water first and disappeared in the fog. Johnson entered the water with an inflated plastic bag, which he intended to use as a flotation device. The cold, rough water immediately proved insurmountable. Johnson realized he could not survive, and immediately returned to the island, where he hid among the large rocks on the beach. As he stated after his capture, "When I got into the water, the bag was torn from my hands and I lost not only the bag, but just about everything I had, including my dental plate." When Miller did not make his periodic report, a search party was organized and he was found within thirty minutes. Johnson was captured a little over an hour later.

An extensive search for Burgett was launched, but no trace of him was found. The search of the bay, particularly around the island, went on for several days, and a national all-points bulletin was issued. On Sunday, October 12, 1958, almost two weeks after his disappearance, the officer on duty in the road tower spotted Burgett's body floating in the bay only a few hundred feet from where he had entered the water. Although the body was severely decomposed and had to be identified by fingerprints, the wooden swim fins were still in place on Burgett's feet.

John Anglin – Clarence Anglin – Frank Morris – Allen West—1962

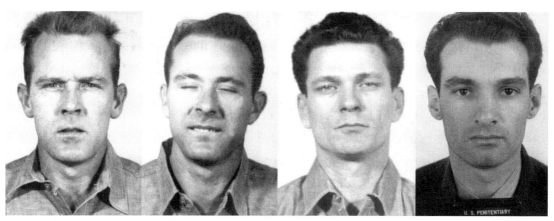

| John Anglin | Clarence Anglin | Frank Morris | Allen West |

John Anglin, Clarence Anglin, and Frank Morris tunneled through the rear walls of their cells and eventually reached the bay with various items of floation equipment. They were never seen again, and are presumed to have drowned. Allen West was part of the plan, but at the last minute, did not leave his cell.

The subject of a movie made in 1973, the escape of June 11, 1962, is probably the most well-known of all the Alcatraz escape attempts. After months of planning and preparation, Frank Morris, John Anglin, and Clarence Anglin succeeded in enlarging the six-by-nine-inch ventilation openings in the back of their cells, and literally tunneled to freedom. A fourth inmate, Allen Clayton West, was also part of the escape team, but because of a problem that developed at the last minute, was unable to get out of his cell in time to join the others.

Frank Morris is generally credited as being the architect of the escape, although after it was over, West claimed to have been the mastermind. Most investigators have discounted West's claims. Morris lived through a dysfunctional childhood and grew up in foster homes. His first criminal conviction was for burglary when he was thirteen. At fourteen, he went to jail for six years, nine months, again for burglary. In time, his crimes became more serious, and his incarcerations occasionally ended in escape. He escaped from the Louisiana State Penitentiary, and when he attempted to escape from the federal penitentiary in Atlanta, he was sent to Alcatraz.

John and Clarence Alglin were two of fourteen children from a Florida family, and turned to crime early in their lives. Along with their brother Alfred, they robbed a bank in Alabama and, when captured a few days later and convicted, were all sent to the federal prison at Atlanta. Here they met Frank Morris. The brothers were subsequently transferred to Leavenworth, and when they attempted to escape, they were sent to Alcatraz.

West had the distinction of being one of the few Alcatraz prisoners to serve multiple terms on The Rock. He was there from 1954 to 1956, and was serving his second term when he became involved in the 1962 breakout. Born and raised in New York, his criminal exploits included armed robbery and interstate transportation of stolen vehicles. He also had a history of escape, which was part of the reason he was at Alcatraz. While serving time in the Florida State Penitentiary, from which he attempted escape, he became friends with John Anglin. This friendship was renewed once the men were reunited on Alcatraz.

The plan originated when the four discussed the possibility of breaking out of the cellhouse through one of the ventilators in the roof. Once they decided such an exit was possible, the planning moved to a means of getting out of their cells. While experimenting with the concrete walls of their cells, the four convicts discovered that the aging concrete had deteriorated to such an extent that it was possible to dig into the wall using simple tools. Because of this deterioration, they concluded that they could enlarge the six-by-nine-inch, screened ventilation opening in the rear wall of their cells sufficiently to slip through. Once they determined this could be done, they put together and carried out a fantastic escape plan. For weeks, they surreptitiously dug around their ventilation screens, expanding the openings. The concrete spoils were flushed down the toilet or brushed back into the utility corridor behind their cells. To conceal the excavation work, they fabricated false ventilators made of papier maché and cardboard. In time, the openings were large enough for them to crawl through and gain access to the utility corridor behind their cells. Their work was carried on at night after lights out and during quiet periods when cellhouse supervision was reduced.

Once they were able to leave their cells, they began constructing the equipment they would need during the escape. From the utility corridor behind their cells, they climbed to the top of the tier and carried on their preparation high above the cellhouse floor. They also worked for weeks cutting through the bolts that held a ventilator in place in the ceiling of the cellhouse. They were able to reach the underside of the ventilator from the top of the cellblock. It was estimated that twenty or more inmates assisted the four in gathering materials, tools, and equipment.

Morris was an inmate painter and was able to convince the administration that the upper part of the cellblock needed painting. Blankets were hung around the work area, ostensibly to prevent paint chips from falling during the scraping phase of the work. In reality, the blankets served as a shield for the escape preparations. The scraping and painting project dragged on for months, while at night behind the blanket shrouds, the inmates were preparing for their escape.

To hide their absence at night while they were working outside their cells, they fabricated heads made of soap, rags and other materials painted in flesh tones and topped with hair obtained from the barbershop. The heads, along with pillows and clothing, were placed under blankets on their bunks to make it appear the men were sleeping when the hourly counts were made during the night. Using as many as fifty raincoats, they constructed life jackets, a six-by-fourteen-foot raft, and other flotation devices. They also built a wooden paddle and a crude flashlight. Morris removed the bellows from his concertina, which they planned to use to inflate the raft once they got to the water. One of the most difficult aspects of the preparation was cutting through the ventilator in the ceiling. By using various tools and parts of hacksaw blades that they were able to commandeer from various locations and individuals, they eventually succeeded in cutting through the ventilator.

The escape from the cellhouse commenced immediately after lights out at 9:30 p.m. The dummy heads were placed in the bunks, and three of the men left their cells, meeting at the top of the cellblock. West later claimed he was unable to get his fake ventilator out of the opening and was unable to join the other three. Some have suggested that he lost his nerve at the last minute and decided to abandon the escape plan. Once through the ventilator opening in the ceiling, they crossed the prison's roof, then climbed down a fifty-foot length of pipe to the ground. They apparently entered the water at the northeastern corner of the island somewhere near the powerhouse.

The plan was to proceed to Angel Island, approximately two miles to the northeast. There, they would rest before crossing Raccoon Straits to Marin County. Once in Marin, it was their plan to steal a car, then burglarize a clothing store for civilian clothing. Thereafter they would split up and each go his separate way. The three inmates have never been seen since, nor have any of them been heard from. The investigation into the escape went on for months, and speculation has persisted for decades as to whether any of the men survived. It is generally surmised that all three men perished.

While there is no evidence that the men survived, there is considerable evidence suggesting they did not. The tide was running out that night, which would carry the bodies quickly out to sea. At approximately the same time the convicts were attempting to make the crossing from Alcatraz, a man committed suicide by jumping off the Golden Gate Bridge. Despite the fact that his suicide was witnessed by scores of people and the Coast Guard was notified immediately, his body was never recovered. The temperature of San Francisco Bay averages about fifty-three degrees Fahrenheit and can produce serious symptoms of hypothermia within as little as twenty minutes to someone unfamiliar with cold-water swimming. One of the life jackets was found deflated about fifty yards from Alcatraz. The large raft was never found, either in the water on on land. One of the smaller rafts was found deflated near Angel Island and the makeshift oar was found in the same general area. A watertight container containing several personal items belonging to Clarence Anglin, as well as money, was found several days after the men disappeared. Investigation revealed that no cars had been stolen and no clothing stores burglarized in Marin County during a twelve-day period following the breakout.

Of great significance to those who believe that the men did not survive was the July 17, 1962, sighting of a body at sea by the S.S. *Norefjell*, a Norwegian freighter. One of the ship's lookouts observed a body floating face down in the water about twenty miles northwest of the Golden Gate Bridge, and the sighting was detailed in the ship's log. The body appeared to be wearing denim trousers similar to the Alcatraz prison uniform. The body matched no missing person report.

Darl Dee Parker – John Paul Scott—1962

Darl Dee Parker   John Paul Scott

John Paul Scott and Darl Dee Parker cut through the bars on a kitchen window and made their way to the water. Parker, cold and frightened, took refuge on a nearby rock and was captured, but Scott floated all the way to the base of the Golden Gate Bridge. Although technically Scott escaped to the mainland, he was so hypothermic that he required hospitalization.

The final escape attempt took place in December 1962, when Darl Dee Parker and John Paul Scott cut through a barred window of the kitchen and eventually made it to the water. While their escape attempt was no more successful than the previous thirteen, it was the first time an Alcatraz convict was known to have reached the mainland alive. This escape, coupled with the escape of six months earlier, clearly established that Alcatraz was no longer the heralded escape-proof bastille it had been for so many years.

Parker arrived at Alcatraz in May 1959, serving fifty years for armed robbery and escape. With his lengthy sentence, a history of escape, and the admission to the warden at the federal penitentiary at Terre Haute, Indiana, that he would try to escape at the first opportunity, it was felt that Parker required maximum security.

Scott did not seem to fit the profile of a career criminal. He was from a caring and loving family. His father was the postmaster in Springfield, Kentucky, and his mother never worked outside the home. By all reports, his mother and father were excellent parents. Young Scott graduated from high school and enrolled at the University of Kentucky, where he maintained an above-average academic standing. He also attended the University of Georgia, Georgia State University, and Western State Teachers College, and served honorably in the United States Air Force. Despite what seemed to be multiple opportunities to lead a productive life, Scott turned to crime.

He was first arrested at the age of twenty-two for possession of stolen property. Thereafter, he was convicted of other crimes including burglary and armed robbery. In January 1957, he and two accomplices held up a bank in Campton, Kentucky, and during their getaway, engaged in a shootout with bank guards and local police. Scott was wounded. He was sent to Atlanta following his conviction and after an escape attempt, he was transferred to Alcatraz in 1959.

Parker and Scott had worked in the kitchen for approximately eighteen months before the escape attempt. During that time, they had cut through the bars of one of the windows using butcher's twine soaked in wax, then covered with scouring powder. They also employed a serrated spatula to cut the bars. They worked on the bars for nearly a year. Apparently a former inmate had started cutting on the bar, and when he was transferred to another facility, the two picked up where he had left off. When they were ready to go, they waited for a Sunday and the last count of the day. This, they hoped, would be the quietest time to make their break.

They greased their bodies with lard from the kitchen to facilitate slipping through the opening left by the missing bar. Once on the ground, they climbed to the roof of the prison, crossed to the other side on the roof, and let themselves back down to the ground using an electrical cord they had stolen. They then worked their way to the northwest corner of the island below the industrial area, where they entered the water. The simple but ingenious flotation system they used made it possible for Scott to float all the way to the Golden Gate Bridge.

As part of their plan, they had accumulated several pairs of rubber gloves from the hospital. Just before entering the water they inflated the gloves and tied them off at the wrists. They stuffed the inflated rubber gloves into their pants and shirts, providing considerable buoyancy. Parker, cold and frightened by the choppy water, took refuge on Little Alcatraz, about two hundred yards west of the prison. Scott, on the other hand, swam out into the shipping channel and was picked up by the outgoing tide. He swam and floated all the way to the Golden Gate just below Fort Point. By the time he reached Fort Point, Scott was suffering serious hypothermia and shock and was barely conscious. He managed to hold onto a large rock or he would have been swept out to sea. Two boys playing in the area spotted Scott, and notified the Presidio military police. The prisoner was rescued and taken immediately to the Presidio's Letterman Hospital in hypothermic shock. Although technically Scott had escaped from Alcatraz, his was not a capture, but a rescue. When well enough to travel, he was returned to Alcatraz, where he and Parker remained in isolation until the prison closed three months later, on March 21, 1963.

Chapter XIII

The Battle of Alcatraz

May 2, 1946, witnessed the most sensational event in Alcatraz history, when six inmates staged the island's most violent and bloody escape attempt. The prisoners managed to invade the west gun gallery, obtain guns, take hostages, and control the entire cellhouse. It took the better part of three days, thousands of rounds of gunfire, rifle grenades, and World War II SHAPE bombs to finally put down the assault. I don't remember what the acronym SHAPE stood for, but it described a weapon used to penetrate concrete enemy bunkers in the Pacific during World War II. What I do remember is that those weapons, although effective against the Japanese on Iwo Jima and Okinawa, could not penetrate the steel and concrete of Alcatraz. In addition to the military explosives, a contingent of battle-hardened marines just back from the war took part in quelling the uprising. By the time it was over, five men lay dead—three inmates and two officers. Fifteen officers and one inmate were wounded. That Thursday, Friday, and Saturday in May 1946 have been acknowledged by historians as one the most noteworthy events in San Francisco history.

The escape attempt was planned and directed by Kentucky bank robber Bernard Coy. The product of a violent and unhappy home, Coy had been a criminal since childhood and was serving twenty-five years for bank robbery. Co-conspirator, and co-leader was former Public Enemy #5, thirty-five-year-old Joseph Cretzer *(described in Chapter XII)*.

Marvin Hubbard was a major participant. Born and raised in the backwoods of Alabama, he was serving thirty years for robbery and kidnapping. His criminal history began during the depths of the Depression; he could not find work as a brick-layer and turned to crime. His background included many shoot-outs, jailbreaks, and violent crimes.

Miran Thompson, a small-time hold-up man who staged robberies through-out the southern states, was also a member of the group. He arrived at Alcataz in November 1945, serving ninety-nine years for kidnapping and murdering a police inspector in Amarillo, Texas. Within weeks of his arrival on The Rock, he began establishing himself as someone with the interest and courage to break out of Alcatraz. As a "cop killer," he was highly regarded in the general population.

Clarence Carnes was a nineteen-year-old Choctaw Indian born and raised on a reservation near Atoka, Oklahoma. When he was only sixteen, he killed a service station attendant during an armed robbery and, upon conviction, received a life sen-tence. Following an abortive escape attempt from the Oklahoma State Reformatory, he received a sentence of ninety-nine years for a kidnapping associated with the escape attempt. At the age of eighteen, serving a sentence of life plus ninety-nine years and having a history of escape attempts, Carnes was sent to Alcatraz, making him the youngest man to do time on the island prison .

The final participant in the breakout attempt was Sam Shockley. Given his condition of mental retardation and paranoid schizophrenia, it is unlikely that "Crazy Sam" was part of the original plan. Once the escape attempt got underway, Shockley's D Block cell was opened, and he joined the group. During the entire event, he was little more than a cheerleader.

Almost from the day he arrived at Alcatraz, Coy discussed with others the possibility of escape. Early in his planning, he dismissed any thought of swimming to freedom, correctly concluding that method was bound to fail. Instead, he deter-mined that a successful escape could only be accomplished by using the island motor launch, the *McDowell*, as the getaway vehicle.

To escape on the boat, he required certain things. The key to the boat was in the custody of the dock tower officer, so Coy concluded he would need hostages to trade for the key. Since getting to the dock from the cell house involved passing under towers manned by heavily armed guards, Coy believed that he needed firearms to neutralize the fire power of the tower guards. He further determined

Bernard Coy, the ringleader of the sensational and bloody escape attempt of May 2, 1946.

Bernard Coy

Miran Thompson, Clarence Carnes, and Marvin Hubbard, along with Joseph Cretzer and Sam Shockley, joined Coy in the May 1946 break-out attempt.

Miran Thompson   Clarence Carnes   Marvin Hubbard

that the only realistic source of guns was in the cellhouse. The island's guns could be found in the armory, the various towers, the top of the yard wall, and the gun galleries in the cellhouse. Access to all those locations except the gun galleries was impossible, so Coy decided that the cellhouse guns would be his target. There were two gun galleries in the cellhouse, the east and the west. Both ran the entire width of the cellhouse, and consisted of two levels connected by ladders. They overlooked the entire cellhouse and the officer on duty in each gallery was armed.

The east gallery was only manned when all the prisoners were in their cells. The west gallery, on the other hand, was manned twenty-four hours a day by an officer who carried a semi-automatic Colt .45 pistol and a .30-06 Springfield bolt-action rifle. All the cellhouse keys were stored in the west gallery and passed down to the cellhouse officers as needed. One of these keys, #107, opened the door leading from the cellhouse to the recreation yard. Coy believed that if he could get into the west gun gallery, overpower the officer on duty, and get his guns and keys, he would have taken the first steps toward freedom.

The next step would involve access to the recreation yard. There, with the element of surprise and his firepower, he could shoot the officer on the yard wall and in the nearby road tower and gain possession of their weapons. Each of those officers carried not only a pistol and rifle, but a Thompson submachine gun. Once in the yard, then through the yard wall gate, it would be an easy trip to the dock, where the hostages would be exchanged for the boat key. The inmates would then be on their way to freedom with a significant arsenal of weapons. To confuse the tower guards, Coy planned to dress the hostages in prison garb, with the prisoners wearing the officers' uniforms.

Although the plan seemed sound in Coy's mind, the mechanics of getting into the gun gallery and obtaining the guns would not be easy. Since Coy was convinced that any escape had to originate in the cellhouse, he obtained employment as a library orderly during the morning hours and worked as a cleanup orderly during the afternoon. These work assignments allowed him to be in the cellhouse all day, yet out of his cell and free to move around. During this time, he studied the operation of the cellhouse, and the habits and idiosyncrasies of the various officers, all the time searching for a method of breaking into the gun gallery. During his years as a cellhouse orderly, Coy established himself as a model prisoner. He followed directions, did a thorough and conscientious job on every assignment given him, and gained the trust and confidence of the officers. In time, the officers trusted him even if they didn't know exactly where in the cellhouse he was. His reputation was that he was always working and always doing the right thing.

Coy solved the entry problem when he observed a defect in the bar structure of the west gun gallery. He noticed that the vertical bars rose from the floor of the lower tier to a point seven or eight feet above the floor of the upper tier. At that point the bars curved over the top of the upper tier and were embedded in the concrete wall on which the gallery was mounted. Every two feet or so along the length of the bars, a horizontal bar strengthened the vertical bars. His key observation was that at the point where the bars curved, there was no horizontal bar. There was a horizontal bar below the curve and one above the curve, but none at the point of the curvature. This would be the weakest point in the structure, and Coy believed that if he could get a bar-spreader into that point, he could widen the space sufficiently to gain entry to the upper level of the gallery. Once he made this discovery, his plans went full speed ahead, and the details of the escape attempt were put together.

He designed a bar spreader and had a friend who worked in the machine shop construct it for him. It was a simple screw jack consisting of a bolt, a nut, and a steel sleeve that fit over the bolt. A notch in one end of the sleeve and in the opposite end of the bolt allowed the device to fit snugly against the two bars to be moved. Turning the bolt with a pair of long-handled pliers would cause the sleeve to move in one direction and the bolt in the opposite direction, thereby spreading the bars. He concluded that if he moved each bar, one inch there would be room for him to slip through.

Once constructed, the bar spreader was smuggled into the cellhouse, one piece at a time, in the false bottom of a garbage can. The individual pieces were moved surreptitiously from the machine shop to the garbage dumping area, then into the kitchen. Here, one of the inmate plumbers took custody of the parts and hid them with the plumbing tools in the C Block utility corridor until the time they were to be used. A bag of heavy lubricating grease was smuggled into the cellhouse from the industrial area and stored with the bar spreader. Coy would smear the grease over his upper body as lubrication to make it easier for him to slip through the bars.

There remained the major problem of gaining entry to the gallery without being seen by an officer on the floor of the cellhouse or the man on duty in the gallery itself. Coy observed that every day about 1:30 p.m., Bert Burch, the west gun gallery officer, would move to the D Block side of the gallery for twenty to thirty minutes. The gallery went through the wall between the main cellhouse and D block, and along the west and south walls of D Block. A soundproof door separated the two sections of the gallery. That meant that, for twenty or thirty minutes each afternoon, the gun gallery officer was in D Block where he could not see or hear what was going on in the cellhouse. During that same twenty-to thirty-minute period, there was only one officer on the floor of the cellhouse.

After years of dreaming and planning, Coy had everything in place and ready to go by May 2, 1946. Unfortunately for me, I was the officer in charge of the cellhouse at that time. My assistant, Bill Miller, normally took his lunch break before the inmates were fed their noon meal. I went to lunch about 1:30 after all the inmates had eaten and returned to their various work sites for the afternoon. It was one of the quietest periods during the day, and a logical time for only one officer to be on duty on the cellhouse floor. There was also an officer in the kitchen, one in the hospital, one in D Block, one in the west gun gallery, and one in the basement, which the administration deemed adequate. It was while I was at lunch that the planned escape got underway. I brought my lunch from home, and ate in the office area of the cellhouse, rather than in the cell block area.

Before I left for lunch, I had a brief discussion with Coy. I pointed out that Broadway had become a little scuffed up by foot traffic and told him to buff the floor that afternoon. It was about a one-hour job, so he'd still be working on it when I got back from lunch. But when I left the cellhouse, Coy signaled to Hubbard in the kitchen area that I was gone. As a kitchen worker, Hubbard had his afternoons free to either stay in his cell or go to the recreation yard. On Coy's signal, Hubbard returned to the cellhouse from the kitchen to begin his free afternoon. While Officer Miller was giving Hubbard a routine shakedown search for contraband, Coy attacked him from behind, pinning his arms to his sides. Hubbard slugged him several times on the jaw, rendering him unconscious. They removed his uniform, obtained his keys, tied his hands, and put him in the end cell of C Block.

Coy then opened the cells of the inmates who were to join the escape, and with Miller's keys, opened the door to the C Block utility corridor. After retrieving the bar spreader, pliers, and grease, he stripped off his clothes and smeared grease over the upper part of his body. He then scrambled up the front of the gallery to the point where the bars curved toward the wall. With help from Hubbard, he spread the bars and slipped into the top level of the gallery. He descended the ladder to the lower level and waited at the door to D Block. When Officer Burch returned a few minutes later, Coy overpowered him, knocked him unconscious, removed his uniform, and tied him up. He obtained the officer's guns and passed them down to his confederates on the cellhouse floor. He scooped up all the keys stored in the gallery as well as billy clubs, gas masks, and gas billies. The latter weapon was a billy club that could dispense tear gas. He passed all these items, including Burch's uniform, to the men below. By this time, Thompson, Carnes, and Cretzer had joined Hubbard below the gun gallery. Coy then climbed out of the gallery and returned to the cellhouse floor.

Upon receiving the guns, Cretzer and Hubbard invaded D Block and captured Officer Cecil Corwin, the officer in charge there. They attempted to release inmate Rufus "Whitey" Franklin, an expert with both weapons and locks, to join them, but he was in one of the solitary confinement cells. The doors to these cells were controlled from the gun gallery and the inmates didn't know how to open Franklin's cell. They next captured Officer Joe Burdett, the kitchen officer, and the chief steward, Bob Bristow. All of the captured officers were placed in cell #404, the end cell of C Block.

When I returned from lunch, I spoke briefly with another of the orderlies, Thomas Wareagle, then observed a couple of strange things. In the first place, Coy had not waxed the floor of Broadway as I had instructed him, which was highly unusual. I also noticed a number of men standing at the far end of Broadway, which was also unusual. I ran down to Time Square to see what was going on and ran straight into Coy and Cretzer holding guns. I was captured and placed in cell #404 along with the others. Shortly after I was placed in the cell, Bill Miller asked Carnes if someone could untie his hands. Without hesitation, he and Cretzer agreed, and we untied Miller. With his hands freed, Miller reached in his shirt pocket and removed key #107. He handed it to Burdett, and whispered, "Here, Joe, hide this someplace. Without this, those assholes aren't going anywhere." Unobtrusively, Burdett slipped the key behind the wall-mounted table near the back of the cell. Coy wanted to the lock the door of cell #404 but was unable to do so. He moved the five of us to the next cell, 403, which could be locked.

Key #107, like all the cellhouse keys, was kept in the gun gallery and passed down to the cellhouse officer when the door to the yard had to be opened. As soon as the door was closed and locked, the key was to be returned to the gallery until it was needed again. Key #107 and the other cellhouse keys passed from the gallery to the floor and back via a rope-and-pulley device operated by the gallery officer. On this day, however, Miller did not send key #107 up to the gallery, but put it in his shirt pocket, since he would be opening and closing the door frequently as the kitchen workers went to and from the yard during the afternoon.

As Coy and Hubbard sorted through the keys, searching for the elusive key #107, Cretzer stood in front of the cell. Over the years, we had become friends because of our association in D Block. For a time, he was the D Block orderly, and I was the officer in charge of D Block. Cretzer was a well-read, intelligent man, and we spent a lot of time discussing many subjects. He enjoyed our "bull sessions," as he referred to them, in part because I respected his opinions even when they differed from mine.

Taking advantage of our relationship and the obvious consternation created by their inability to find the key, I attempted to convince Cretzer of the futility of the venture and the wisdom of surrendering before anyone got hurt. But Joe was wild with anticipation, and would have none of my suggestion. "No, Mr. Lageson," he responded politely, "This ain't one of our bull sessions. This is the real thing, and we're going. You're a good guy, and I hope you don't get hurt, but we're going."

In the basement of the cell house, Officer Ed Stucker was supervising twenty-some inmates taking showers, getting haircuts, receiving clean clothes and linens, and various other activities. As part of his duties, he went upstairs and checked the cellhouse. Things didn't look right, so he called the armory officer, Cliff Fish, expressing his concern. In response to Stucker's call, Fish called all the cellhouse duty stations, but none of his calls was answered. As Fish was trying to determine the status of things in the cellhouse, Captain Henry Weinhold returned from lunch. Upon learning of the problem, he rushed into the cell block area and was captured. Over the next several minutes Lieutenant Joe Simpson and Officers Bob Baker and Carl Sundstrom went to the aid of the captain and were also captured. The nine hostages were placed in two empty cells, six men in #403 and three in #402

During this time, the inmates were trying the various keys taken from the gun gallery, puzzled by the fact that key #107 was not there and none of the other keys would open the door to the yard. The inmates knew that key #107 opened that door, but it never occurred to them that Miller would have kept the key in his possession rather than sending it up to the gallery. That was in violation of prison regulations, something none of them considered. The failure of the inmates to obtain that critical key effectively ended the escape attempt. Since they could not get out of the cellhouse, the guns and hostages did them no good. As the convicts considered their options, Officer Fish and others concluded there was an escape attempt in progress and the alarm was sounded.

Captain Weinhold tried to talk Cretzer into surrendering. He pointed out to the now-confused inmate that with the alarm sounding all the off-duty officers would be at the cellhouse in a matter of minutes and they would all be armed. He admonished Cretzer that there was absolutely no chance of success, and he would be wise to give up before anyone was killed or injured. "Look, Joe," the captain warned, "even if you find the key to the outside door, the first man to step out there will be the first man to die."

"No, Captain," Cretzer sneered, "you'll be the first man to die."

"Well, you can only die once," Weinhold fearlessly responded.

With no further comment Cretzer shot the captain at point-blank range in the chest, and Weinhold sank unconscious to the floor. Cretzer then fired randomly into the cell, sending bullets ricocheting in all directions. He then moved to cell #402 and shot the officers there. Having been one of the first men to enter cell #403, I was seated at the rear of the cell. When the shooting was over, the other five officers in my cell were sprawled all over the floor, and all appeared lifeless. I had not been hit, but unfortunately, I also had nowhere to go. There was no place on the floor to play dead, and before I had time to do much of anything, Shockley spotted me.

"Hey, Joe! There's a son-of-a-bitch in the corner that's still alive. Kill him."

Cretzer looked into the cell and saw me. "Naw, that's Mr. Lageson. He's a good guy and always treated me right. He's my friend."

"Friend, hell!" Thompson protested. "He'll testify against us. He'll go to court and screw us all. Kill him. We don't want no witnesses. If you don't want to kill him, Joe, give me the gun and I will."

Cretzer was clearly in a dilemma. If he didn't shoot me, one of the others would, and he'd lose face in the eyes of his fellow convicts. Yet he had announced to Hubbard when the escape alarm sounded: "Well, Marv, Frisco's as far away as ever, and I'm going the hard way." Cretzer intended to die in the upcoming shoot-out, and he would never stand trial for anything.

"Mr. Lageson, I'm really sorry about this," he said almost in a whisper. He steadied the barrel of the pistol on one of the crossbars of the cell and aimed the gun at me. I asked God to look after Eunice and Little Ernie and waited to die. When Cretzer squeezed the trigger, the hammer snapped harmlessly against the empty bullet chamber. The gun was empty. He pulled out the spent clip and rammed another clip of seven bullets into the grip of the pistol. He pulled the slide back, cocking the gun and pointed it at me once again. The only sound was the wail of the siren outside as the other inmates watched Cretzer. This time when he squeezed the trigger, the gun thundered and I was unconscious.

My next awareness was of slowly regaining consciousness, still seated, but pitched forward with my head between my legs. Everything was hazy, like being in a dream, and I was disoriented. As my mind began to, clear, I recalled Cretzer with the gun and I wondered if I was dead. It was a strange sensation. I was aware of a throbbing pain on the left side of my face. I felt dizzy, like I was floating, then I lost consciousness again.

I had no idea how much time passed until I regained consciousness. This time my mind was totally clear and I was immediately aware of the horrible situation I was in. I could hear the voices of the inmates in the distance, but there didn't seem to be anyone standing directly in front of the cell. There was a small puddle of blood at my feet from the wound in my face, and I was experiencing a lot of pain. I wondered how much of my face had been torn away. I carefully ran my fingers over the wound and confirmed that my face was still there. The left side of my face was numb to the touch, yet painful, and there was blood on my fingers. I lifted my head slightly so I could look around the cell and see the other officers. None of them were moving, and I assumed they were all dead.

I strained to hear the inmate conversation coming from the end of the cell-block. They were still trying to open the door to the yard, and I could hear the rattle of keys. Then I heard Hubbard order Carnes to come and check on us. "Hey, kid, go check the screws and make sure they're all dead. If any of them are still alive, use this—we don't want to waste any more bullets on 'em." I learned later the "this" to which he referred was a 12-inch carving knife he had brought from the kitchen.

Carnes came to the front of the cell and paused, apparently checking on whether any of us were still alive. I sat there motionless, holding my breath, my head between my legs. He walked to the next cell, then back to the end of the tier and reported to Hubbard, "They're all dead, Marv. They're all just like we left 'em."

Knowing that there was no one in front of the cell, I raised up again and looked around. I carefully observed Corwin, Miller, and the captain and could see that, while unconscious, they were all breathing. Bristow was under the bunk and out of sight. Burdett was sprawled across the bunk, half on and half off with his head near mine. Moving as close to him as I could, I whispered into his ear, "Are you okay, Joe?"

"Yeah, Ernie, I'm fine. How are the others?"

"Corwin, Weinhold, and Miller are alive, but they've been shot bad. I don't know about Bristow."

"I'm okay," Bristow whispered from under the bed.

We maintained our positions for what seemed like an eternity. From time to time, the prisoners would come to front of the cell to check if any of us had moved. While I had survived Cretzer's volley of gunfire, I doubted that I would survive the evening. The unconscious men were clearly breathing, and if the prisoners observed that, they would surely come into the cells and kill us all. For that reason, during one of the quiet periods while they were not observing us, I wrote the names of the six inmates involved on the wall of the cell. If we didn't survive, it would be evidence for the investigators as to who had killed us. I circled the names of Coy and Hubbard since they were the ones who overpowered Miller at the beginning. Since Cretzer was the shooter, I circled his name and put a check after it.

In time, I heard shots being fired down "Seedy Street," the corridor between C and D Blocks, and a flurry of activity by the convicts. The east gun gallery had obviously been manned, and the officers were firing at the cons when they came into the corridor. From the east gun gallery, there was a clear view of Seedy Street and by standing in front of our cell, the prisoners now risked getting shot. That gunfire and those ricocheting bullets were really welcome sounds, for now there would be no one checking on us. Then we heard the prisoners take refuge in the utility corridor behind the rear wall of our cells. We still weren't safe, because there was only the wall between us, and their voices were clearly audible through the ventilation opening. We knew we had to be silent for fear they'd hear us and risk coming back to finish us off.

Captain Weinhold, who was unconscious and gravely wounded, began mumbling incoherently, and we feared the inmates would hear him. He was delirious and had obviously lost a lot of blood. He first asked for water, then expressed fear that he would miss his young daughter's birthday party scheduled for that night. In an effort to keep him quiet, we tried giving him water, but that was not easy to do. I ran a little water from the sink into my cupped hand and passed it to Burdett. Joe in turn trickled the water into the captain's mouth. After a few handfuls, he was quiet and we were all able to move about and stretch. Periodically we would repeat the water treatment, which kept the captain comfortable and quiet.

By 7:00 p.m., both gun galleries had been occupied and the inmates were cornered in the utility corridor. Coy, Cretzer, and Hubbard chose to make their final stand in the corridor, while the other three returned to their cells to await their fate. This permitted us considerable freedom to minister to the more seriously wounded men, although we continued to maintain quiet. We could still hear the inmates in the corridor behind us, but were satisfied they no longer presented the life-threatening menace they previously had.

Warden Johnston resisted sending armed officers into the cellhouse to rescue the hostages. Although the associate warden and the lieutenants urged that a rescue party be organized, the warden would not authorize it. He opposed allowing guns on the cellhouse floor, fearing they might fall into the hands of the inmates. With both gun galleries manned by several heavily armed officers, his concern was unrealistic, but the warden was steadfast in his opinion. Finally, at about 10:45, Johnston agreed to let Miller lead an armed party into the cellhouse. By then, the position of the hostages was known, and the rescue operation went smoothly. The four of us who could walk helped carry out the five seriously wounded men, while the rescue party sent a steady stream of gunfire into the upper level of C Block. The

The names of the inmates participating in the 1946 escape attempt, written on the wall of the hostage cell by Officer Ernest Lageson, who believed he would not survive the uprising.

three holdouts had climbed up to the top of the block and initially fired down at the rescue party. Their brief gunfire was met with a fusillade from the officers, forcing the inmates to retreat to their final refuge in the bottom of the C Block utility corridor.

The gunfire went on all night and into the next day. Inmates not involved in the escape were kept in the yard, since the cell house was a war zone. A contingent of marines was sent from the Treasure Island Naval Base to guard the prisoners in the yard. The presence of the marines freed custodial officers for other tasks. The leader of the marine detachment, Warrant Officer Charles Buckner, was a weapons expert. He volunteered to end the holdout using military weapons, and Warden Johnston readily accepted the offer. For much of Friday, Buckner dropped hand grenades, SHAPE bombs, and other explosives into the utility corridor through holes drilled in the roof of the cell house. In addition to the overhead barrage, officers sprayed the corridor with rifle fire. After hours of relentless bombardment and rifle fire, the interior of C Block was silent. Late Saturday morning, a party of officer volunteers entered the corridor and found the bodies of Coy, Cretzer, and Hubbard. They had all died from bullet wounds to the head.

While none of us grieved over the inmate deaths, there was profound sadness over the deaths of the two officers. Shot through the chest and lungs, Officer Bill Miller died Friday morning. Officer Harold Stites, the man who single-handedly ended the escape attempt in 1938, was killed by friendly fire from outside the cell

Bar spreader used by Coy on the bars of the west gun gallery, facilitating his entry into the gallery. Notched ends were placed against the bars, then forced apart by turning the nut with a pair of long-handled pliers. This moved each bar approximately one inch, creating an opening large enough for Coy to slip through.

The utility corridor where Coy, Cretzer and Hubbard died.

Warden Johnston in front of cell #403 following the 1946 escape attempt.

house when he and a group of officers entered the west gun gallery.

Within weeks of the uprising, the three survivors were charged with the murder of Officer Miller. The case went to trial six months later in the federal district court in San Francisco before Judge Louis Goodman. After a month-long trial, all three of the defendants were convicted of first-degree murder. The jury sentenced Shockley and Thompson to death, and Carnes received another life sentence. The latter testified during the trial that he knew we were all alive when he looked into the cell, but lied to Hubbard and the others to save our lives. He told the jury that by then, he knew that the escape attempt had failed, and he saw no reason to kill us. The jury accepted his testimony and showed him leniency. As it turned out, my testimony on that issue was definitive. I had heard Carnes's statements and corroborated his trial testimony. Carnes returned to Alcatraz and served sixteen more years before being transferred to the medical facility at Springfield for gall-bladder surgery. After appellate proceedings upheld their convictions and sentences, Shockley and Thompson were executed in the San Quentin gas chamber in December 1948.

Federal District Judge Louis
Goodman, who presided
over the murder trial of
Carnes, Thompson, and
Shockley.

Clarence Carnes in 1987, at the age
of 60. He died the following year.

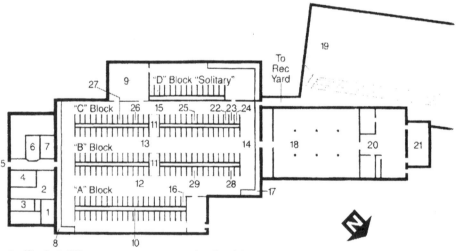

1. Warden's Office
2. Armory
3. Associate Warden's Office
4. Guard's Waiting Room
5. Entrance
6. Control Room
7. Visitation Room
8. East Gun Gallery
9. Library
10. Utility Corridors

11. Cell Cut Offs
12. "Michigan Blvd."
13. "Broadway"
14. "Times Square"
15. "Seedy Street"
16. Coy's Magazine Office
17. West Gun Gallery
18. Dining Hall
19. Recreation Yard
20. Kitchen

21. Bakery
22. Cell #402
23. Cell #403 (Hostage Cells)
24. Cell #404
25. Cretzer's Cell
26. Hamilton's Cell (Middle Tier)
27. Thompson's Cell (Middle Tier)
28. Coy's Cell
29. Carnes' Cell

Cellhouse diagram, May 1946

Inside the west gun gallery looking south toward D Block. Main cellhouse visible to left of bars.

Isolation cell door showing opening through which the food tray was passed.

D Block. The solitary cells are the six cells at the far end of the bottom tier.

Chapter XIV

Outside the Normal Routine

Despite the ever-present tension affecting both convicts and guards, there were also times of humor, pathos, and a myriad of human emotions. While taking each day as it came, and making the most of their shattered lives, many inmates dispensed surprising bits of wisdom and humor. These men made prison work interesting, and left me with lasting memories of our relationships.

"Fats" was one of the most personable inmates on Alcatraz, and despite the fact that he was serving a thirty-two year sentence, he never expressed bitterness or negative feelings. Given the facts of his conviction and sentence, there were few Alcatraz inmates who would have maintained the pleasant outlook exhibited by Fats. While he was on a hunting trip miles from the scene of the crime, the gang of which he was a part hijacked a railroad car load of cigarettes that was moving through interstate commerce. This made the crime a federal offense, and the FBI was on the case. Fats owned a place in the country large enough to store the stolen cigarettes, and without his knowledge or permission, the gang hid the loot there. Fats' wife was apparently aware of the situation, and when the FBI swooped in, she was one of those arrested. To protect her from possible conviction and imprisonment, Fats "took the rap" and ended up in federal prison. His involvement in a major conspiracy at Leavenworth soon after his conviction got him transferred to Alcatraz. From the day he arrived, he stood out as one of the most polite, cooperative, and pleasant inmates on the island. He was soon a favorite of officers and inmates alike.

At the outset, he worked as a cellhouse orderly, but soon requested work in the industries. This was granted, and he went to work in the prison tailor shop. He was given special dispensation by the administration to leave work early each noon and evening, to allow him added time to move his 5ft. 3in., 300-pound frame up the long paths and stairways from the industrial area to the cellhouse. He sought medical care to reduce his weight. While in the tailor shop, he was not content to be simply a machine operator, but made a concerted effort to learn all phases of tailoring. In response to my compliment regarding his hard work, he offered a sound explanation.

"Mr. Lageson, I've got to prepare for the time I get out on the bricks again. Given my size, clothing on the outside will cost me too damn much money. So I figure if I can learn tailoring in here, when I get out I can make a decent living plus make all my own clothes. I'll save a pile of money."

The last I heard, Fats had been transferred to a less restrictive facility, from which he'd been released on parole. Unfortunately, his lifestyle and excessive weight took its toll, and he died shortly after his release. Fats had seen it all, the good life and the bad, the highs and the lows. Despite his confinement, however, he made working at Alcatraz just a little brighter, and I'd like to think his jovial spirit may still haunt the island.

Fred was another man with a bright personality who had learned how to do time successfully. He had excelled in the highly specialized profession of safe cracking, and had a long record of arrests and imprisonment. In prison, he "did his own time." He stayed out of trouble, worked hard, and conformed. As a result, he was liked and well treated by everyone. I never knew what he did to end up on Alcatraz. He was a steady inmate and enjoyed the hard work of a dock crew freight handler. During my assignment as a dock officer, I got to know Fred well and he was always eager to chat one-on-one with me about all sorts of subjects. On one occasion, we were shaking down military laundry when I asked him, "Fred, what would you do if you found a loaded .45 automatic in one of these army uniforms and were able to get it out without being seen?"

"Boss, I'd grab that damned thing as fast as I could and chuck it as far out into the bay as I could. I don't ever want no part of guns. No sir!"

On another occasion, after the freight boat had shoved off from the island and we were securing the area, he remarked with a straight face and a twinkle in his eye, "Damn, there goes another boat and I'm not on it. You know, Boss, I sure do miss a lot of those boats bound for Frisco."

One day during a smoke break, Fred began talking about family life when he was at the height of his criminal career in Chicago. He described what sounded like a happy marriage, but expressed the generalization that "women sure can be crooked." When I challenged his conclusion, he stuck to his opinion and argued, "Boss, I know I'm right, and I'll tell you a story about my wife that proves my point. We were renting this apartment, and it was beginning to look a little shabby. So my wife asked me if I thought the landlord would let us paint the place and deduct the cost from the rent. I told her that would probably work, and suggested she check it out.

"So my wife wrote to the landlord and he agreed to give us a rent credit for our costs if we painted the apartment. It just so happened that I was going out to crack a box in a hardware store that night, so, after I busted the safe, I loaded up on paint and stuff. I got brushes, linseed oil, thinner, and everything we'd need. So my wife painted the apartment, and do you know what, Boss? That cheatin' little woman charged the landlord for every damn drop of that paint and all the other stuff that I stole." Then he broke out laughing, "See, Boss, don't that prove what I said? And you know what else? That little rascal even overcharged the landlord and marked the prices up."

Another inmate member of the dock crew made a lasting impression on me because of what he learned from his Alcatraz incarceration. Charlie was a husky young Italian lad who had seen himself as a "really tough guy" on the outside. One day, after loading a monstrous pile of laundry, Charlie sat down, mopped his brow, and said, "Boy, I sure wish my mother's little boy was home!"

"Well, keep behaving yourself like you've been doing out here," I responded, "and that will happen. How is it that a young guy like you winds up doing twenty-five years, and serving it on Alcatraz?"

"Well, Boss, I thought I was a pretty tough little guy back there on the South Side of Chicago. I traveled with a gang of young hoods that was stickin' up drug stores. Well, we was doing pretty good and everything was going just fine until we robbed a drug store that had a post office substation in it. We didn't know it at the time, but the few bucks that came out of that postal drawer made it a federal crime, and when those G-Men got done with me, I wind up with a twenty-five year bit. But little Charlie was tough and no damned prison was going to break him. They sent me to Leavenworth, and I spent most of my time either in the Hole or in isolation. They finally got tired of fussin' with me and sent me out here to cool my heels on The Rock. Well, sir, when I began lookin' around at these ten- and fifteen-time losers out here, I said to myself, 'Charlie, what's the percentage? Do you want to be like one of these stir bugs livin' from one release to the next, from one conviction to the next?' So I decided to start on my way back, and let me tell you, Boss, if I ever get out of jail, I'm going to get me a job and work for a livin'. I'm gonna marry some nice little Dago gal, raise bambinos, and carry a dinner pail. And I'll tell what else. There ain't gonna be no gun in that pail; it's gonna be full of salami sandwiches."

Charlie did get his transfer to another prison, and we received word that he had been released and enlisted in the army. He was sent to Europe and fought heroically in the Italian campaign during World War II. If he survived the war, I'm sure Charlie did well. He seemed sincere and had obviously learned that he was on a no-win track to oblivion. He had seen the results of a life of crime up close, and concluded it was not where he wanted to be. I liked Charlie a lot, and I sincerely hope he made it.

Little Eddie was a freight handler, a noisier individual I have never known. He spoke louder than any inmate on the dock, but was a hard worker. Despite his constant chatter, he moved hundreds of pounds of laundry a day. Eddie was young with most of his life ahead of him. In Eddie's case, in spite of the time he had spent in medium-custody prisons, and then Alcatraz, he had concluded that most likely he'd always be a thief. He boasted continuously of his criminal exploits and had numerous deals pending for the time he'd be back on the street. One day, as he worked and chattered, he announced the policy he intended to follow when he was back on the street.

"When I get out after this bit, I'm going to be damned sure that if ever I get caught stealin' again, it's going to be a state rap. Those federal judges dish out too damned much time. First off, you got a much better chance of beatin' a state rap, and if you do lose, the time ain't nearly as long." Eddie was transferred while I was still at Alcatraz, and of all the inmates I saw transferred, none seemed as happy as he was.

"What's the difference, Eddie?" I chided, "You're just going to another jail."

"Oh, Boss, there's a big difference. Man oh man, I can buy cigars at the commissary again. And there's not all them damned counts like here on The Rock. You don't know, Boss, but it's just like goin' home."

Eddie, too, had learned from his time on Alcatraz. Whereas Charlie had learned to avoid a future life of crime, Eddie had progressed only as far as avoiding a future life of federal crime. Eddie's education was not yet complete, but moving in the right direction.

Bill was a small, emaciated-looking fellow who, though younger than most of the Alcatraz convicts, had seen the inside of a lot of prisons and jails. He had a peculiar walk and shuffled along like an old man. One day, out of curiosity, I asked him, "Bill, what's the problem with your legs? You're a young guy, but you walk like one of the old guys in here."

"Boss, that's from when I did time in the Deep South," and he cited a notorious southern state penitentiary. "Brother, if you think Alcatraz is rugged, you shoulda' been there. They'd get you up long before daylight and march you out into the cotton field. The guards would be on big old horses roamin' around the field, and each one of 'em carried a whip and a shotgun. A guard would yell at us. 'You see that cotton? That's mine. And do you see that crabgrass? That's yours. Now damn your stinkin' hides, get your crabgrass outta my cotton.' Then he'd crack that whip across your back and yell, 'That's for nothin', now try somepthin'.' I tell you, Boss, it was so tough that I couldn't stand it, so one day I cut the tendons to my feet so I couldn't walk, and they had to put me in the hospital. They fixed me up pretty good, but that's why I walk a little funny now." I don't know whether his story was true or not, but considering the accounts I received from other men who had served time in that same prison, I had no trouble believing him. Everything I ever heard about that penitentiary convinced me it was a place of inhuman treatment, totally unlike the firm but humane conditions at Alcatraz.

Slim, an outstanding artist, was serving time for counterfeiting. Much of his artwork consisted of copying photographs and artwork he found in magazines. On occasion, he would reproduce well-known works of art, and to my untrained eye, the reproductions looked as good as the originals. His work was admired by officers and inmates alike, and it was easy to see how he got into the business of producing phony money. According to those who knew him on the outside, Slim's bogus bills were the best. During a routine cell check one day, I came upon Slim intently working with his oils, and I stopped for a moment to admire his work. "Slim, you really do good work."

"Thanks, Boss, it helps kill a little time."

"You're doing time for counterfeiting, aren't you?"

"That's right."

"Some of the boys in here tell me you used to produce some pretty good money."

"Well, I always thought it was pretty damned good, too, but those T-Men didn't think much of my work. In fact they thought it was so bad that they arrested me for it."

Over the years, a number of brother pairs served time on The Rock. One of the most notable of these was a pair who had been convicted of kidnapping, conspiracy, assault, and narcotics smuggling, and their combined sentences exceeded forty years. Both of the boys were Sicilian aliens who, along with an accomplice, had smuggled a large shipment of narcotics into the United States. The hidden cache had been accidentally found by a disinterested third party, who notified the police. After the discovery, the brothers accused their accomplice of double-crossing them and stealing the drugs. They kidnapped him, then severely beat him. Sam, the older brother, was the least articulate but the most talkative of the two. He was assigned to the officers' mess, which at times was a difficult job. The officers frequently had only a limited amount of time to eat, and demanded more service than Sam was able to provide. He'd do the best he could, but when the demands became too much for him, he'd stand in the middle of the room, throw his hands in the air, and shout in broken English, "Whatta hell you tinka I am. Da Mussolin? You tink I canna do mora dan one ting atta time?" But the officers loved Sam, and were sympathetic to his problems of having to satisfy several diners with conflicting schedules. They knew he tried hard, and appreciated his efforts. They would frequently leave unsmoked cigarettes in the ashtrays for him, one of the few acts of generosity officers could legally perform for deserving prisoners. Those who ate in the officers' dining room felt that Sam alone was worth the price of the meal.

One afternoon, after the kitchen crew had completed their work, they were being searched for contraband as they returned to their cells or went to the yard for the afternoon. The alert kitchen officer had called ahead, informing the cellhouse lieutenant that he believed Sam was smuggling ice cream to his cell, concealed in his pants. Despite Sam's popularity, the lieutenant couldn't let him get away with a clear violation of the rules, so he told him, "Sam, you stand over there at the end of the cell block." Sam complied as the officers and lieutenant completed the shake-down. Long after the shakedown of the other inmates was complete, Sam was still standing there as the officers engaged in a prolonged conversation. In time, as the ice cream melted and began to run down the inside of his pants, Sam realized what was being done to him. Finally, in frustration, he called out, "Okay, Boss, you gotta me! Watta you gonna do, putta me in da Hole?"

The lieutenant quietly scolded Sam for bringing contraband food into the cellhouse. Sam knew the rules, and promised not to do it again. Instead of going to the Hole, he was sent back to his cell to deal with the melted ice cream inside his pants.

Cowboy was doing 199 years for kidnapping and murder. During his stay at Alcatraz, he had found his niche as the yard orderly, and worked hard cleaning the recreation yard of rubbish that collected during weekend activities. He also did an excellent job of maintaining the softball diamond so it was always in the best possible playing condition. Resigned to spending the rest of his life in prison, the rangy Texan was a model prisoner and a pleasant man to be with. I once asked him, "Cowboy, how in the hell did you ever get 199 years? That is a mighty long time."

"Boss," he replied in a serious tone, "I guess the judge figgered I was such a bad-ass son-of-a-bitch that he didn't want me on the streets anymore, but he didn't have the heart to top me [execute me], so they gave me 199 years."

Years earlier, Cowboy had participated in a strike and riot, and as a result had lost 365 days of statutory good time. It was customary for the warden and the bureau to restore lost good time to inmates who demonstrated an improved attitude and were deserving of sentence reduction. This was often done at Christmas, to make the Yuletide season a bit more joyous for those involved. Early one December, Cowboy commented to me with what appeared to be a serious concern. "You know, Boss, I'm really hopin' that the warden gives me back my lost year of good time. I could really use it." Cowboy was then in his mid-fifties and with continued good behavior, would have been eligible for parole after serving 130 years, or when he was about 180 years old. Cowboy needed that year and many more.

One of the more ingenious inmates brought mirth to the office with his application for release on parole. In answering the question, *Why do you make application for parole at this time?* he cogently stated, "I've got a life sentence to do for the State of California, and I would like to get started on it as soon as possible."

While I was assigned to isolation, I spent a lot of time chatting with the inmates, since there was little else to do. With the more articulate men, I would discuss the war, national news, books they had read, stories of their lives, and how they ended up at Alcatraz. Regardless of how serious one of these conversations might become, there was always the possibility of being completely surprised by the course of the discussion. On one such occasion, my discussion with Lloyd Barkdoll turned to the fact that the day before had been my day off.

"So, Mr. Lageson, what did you do on your day off yesterday?"

"Oh, I slept late, went over to town, saw a movie, stopped for a beer, then went to the bank and cashed my paycheck."

At that point, he excitedly interrupted. "So, Boss," he inquired in almost a whisper, "was it a big bank?"

Suspecting what might be coming, I played along. "It was the Day and Night Branch of the Bank of America at Powell and Market Streets. You may remember it from your days in San Francisco."

"Yeah, yeah," he responded, "I remember it, a big granite building. Tell me Boss, did you see any bulls around, you know, bank guards?"

"Well there were a couple of uniformed guards in the lobby area. Why do you ask?"

"What do you think, Boss? How many guys would we need to take it? Would six be enough? Tell you what. I'll get three or four good guys from in here, and you

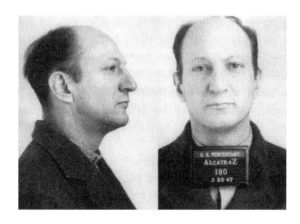

Meloy "Red" Kuykendall had an engaging sense of humor, but a deep hatred for those in law enforcement.

round up a couple of your guard buddies and we'll bust that box wide open, okay?"

And we both laughed. Convict humor shared with a friendly officer had a therapeutic effect in which I was more than happy to participate. It was good for morale, and served to bond inmate and officer.

One day, I walked past Red Kuykendall's cell and observed him stretching and yawning. In jest, I told him he looked like he needed more sleep and should probably go to bed earlier.

"Well, Boss," he responded, "I prefer to stay home at night, listen to the radio, read the paper and get to bed early, but Joe down the gallery drags me over to Frisco every night to go drinkin' and partyin'. You know, at my age, I just can't handle all that tom-cattin' around."

But behind his humor lurked a far different man. Meloy "Red" Kuykendall had a violent escape history, and was considered one of the fiercest and most dangerous convicts at Alcatraz. Most of the time, he was a courteous and able worker. However, I once saw him during in an interview with two FBI special agents, and his vile, vituperative language and his animosity toward the agents exceeded anything I had ever seen or heard. He really hated cops.

Bill Dainard, a notorious kidnapper, was in isolation for manufacturing two pistols in the machine shop. He was serving a sentence of sixty years and had numerous detainers against him filed by jurisdictions around the country. During a one-on-one conversation, Bill came across as an articulate and personable fellow. He was, however, among the prison's most dangerous inhabitants. As mentioned earlier, his partner in his final kidnapping caper was also in D Block, and the two continued to maintain a close relationship. During part of the time I worked in isolation, this ingenious "gunsmith" was my mess orderly, delivering food to the individual cells. Following each meal, and after all utensils were gathered and accounted for, Bill enjoyed chatting with me before being returned to his cell. During one of these chats, it was brought home to me just how small the world was.

"What part of the country are you from?" he inquired.

"North Dakota."

"Really," he responded excitedly, "I was born in North Dakota. Do you know of a place called Cando?"

"I sure do. I taught school about ten miles from there back in the thirties."

"Well, my folks used to live in Considine."

Considine was a whistlestop village a few miles north of Cando, with little more than a grain elevator and a few other buildings. During the course of our conversation, we discovered many families and individuals that we knew in common. I was stunned by the bizarre irony of our paths, which began in rural North Dakota and crossed in the isolation block of Alcatraz.

"The story was that you fellows netted $200,000 in ransom from that snatch, is that correct?" I asked.

"That's right, Mr. Lageson, and let me tell you a story about that dough. After we met for the split, I took my share and checked into a cheap, out-of-the-way-hotel for the night. I dumped the money out on the bed, and I'm tellin' you, Boss, that much money all in one place kinda' scared me. I'd never seen anything like it. A hundred grand in small bills spread out like that looked like a pile of North Dakota alfalfa."

An unfortunate sidelight of Bill's story came out of his choice of an alias during the ransom negotiations. He identified himself as Bill Mahan, and an all-points bulletin was issued for his capture. It so happened that a man named Bill Mahan lived in Cando at the time, and was well-known in the small community. When the police announced that Bill Mahan from Cando was wanted for kidnapping, it became big news; the newspapers statewide were emblazoned with his name. It was devastating for the real Bill Mahan, and it took months for the truth to clear his name. I was teaching in the county at the time, and never dreamed I would someday be one of the custodians of that wanted kidnapper.

"Why did you pick that name as an alias?" I inquired.

"Oh, I don't know. No particular reason. I had heard the name and thought it would be as good as any other. Sure did kick up a lot of fuss though, didn't it?"

When he was arrested nearly a year after the crime, Bill had spent a considerable amount of the money. He was arrested in a parking lot in San Francisco, and it was with some professional embarrassment that he revealed the facts of his arrest.

"I knew I was getting hot, so I carried two guns on me wherever I went. But those G-Men moved in on me so fast that I never had a chance to reach for either of them."

During my tour of duty in the Carpentry Shop, the work of Blackie Audette stood out above his contemporaries both in quality and quantity. One day I observed him fabricate a table leg on the lathe, and the finished product was excellent.

"That's really a fine job you're doing," I said.

"Oh, it'll do," he responded casually as he inspected his work with the practiced eye of an artisan.

"You could make good money doing this on the outside."

"Yeah, I s'pose so," mused Blackie as he continued to study the now finished piece.

"Did you do any of this before you were in prison?"

"Nope, learned it all in jail."

"When you get out, do suppose you'd try to get into this line of work?"

"Naw, I reckon I'll go right back to robbin' banks."

That was the philosophy of so many of the men at Alcatraz. They were what they were, and most had little idea of changing. They harbored the hope of making that big strike and not getting caught. It was always one final big job that would "put them on easy street" and take care of them for the rest of their lives. But the big payday never came. Instead it was a fatal shoot-out with the police or long years in prison, yet few of them ever learned that.

Blackie was an excellent inmate, and had the respect of the custodial force. Not only did he do excellent work, but he also followed the rules. He also had the respect of most of the inmates, although a few distrusted him because he stayed out

Theodore "Blackie" Audette was the only inmate to serve three separate terms on Alcatraz for three separate convictions. At Alcatraz, he was always a model prisoner.

of trouble and was cooperative. He later took a job in the culinary department as a cook, and it was during that time that I was able to take advantage of his popularity and respect among the other inmates to help a fellow officer. The regulation uniform of the mess hall workers was a white shirt and blue trousers instead of the one-piece coverall worn by the other inmates. It was not too surprising, therefore, that occasionally white dress shirts belonging to officers found their way from the civilian laundry into the kitchen. Apparently Arrow and Manhattan shirts fit the inmates better than the shirts produced by the prison clothing shop. When one of the new officers complained to me that all his white dress shirts had disappeared after he sent them to the laundry and asked my advice, I thought of Blackie. I told the young man he could report the loss and would probably get some reimbursement, but I doubted that he'd get his shirts back. "But before you do anything," I suggested, "let me try something."

The next time I saw Blackie, I told him the story, and asked him if he would help the young officer get his shirts back. "He's new, Blackie, and is a real nice guy. He's certainly not making any trouble for you guys in the kitchen, so could you look into it for me and see what you can do?"

"You got it, Boss!" Blackie got the job done, and within a couple of days the shirts, neatly laundered and ironed, were delivered to the officer's room at the bachelor officers' quarters. When I next saw him, Blackie gave me a wink and a nod of his head signifying that the case was closed.

Blackie made good on his announced intention to return to his old ways after release from prison. He earned the dubious distinction of becoming the only inmate in Alcatraz history to serve three separate terms on The Rock. As inmate number 208, his first term for bank robbery started in 1934. He was eventually discharged, but came back to The Rock as number 551 in 1941. He was serving ten years, again for robbery, and it was during that term that I met him. In 1956, Blackie was back in the middle of San Francisco Bay, this time as inmate number 1217 doing another twenty years. There are those who described Blackie as a slow learner.

For some time prior to the final discharge of an inmate, preparations were made for his release. He was measured for a prison-made suit and overcoat (if he was being discharged to a cold climate), his teeth were checked, and he received a complete medical examination. Most of those being released were jumpy and nervous for weeks before their final day, and some even asked to be placed in isolation or on idle status to avoid any possible difficulty that might jeopardize their approaching freedom.

One such convict, called Hank, had been in jail a long time and had become a cool, hardened inmate able to handle any situation presented to him. Yet despite his toughness, as his day of discharge approached, Hank was just like all the rest, full of anxieties and concerns. He had been sentenced in 1919 and was being discharged in 1943, and I could sense his apprehension during those final few weeks. Hank had always felt comfortable confiding in me, and one day when were alone, he began talking about his upcoming release.

"You know, Boss, things have changed an awful lot in twenty-four years, and I'm gettin' kinda' scared about this whole deal."

While counseling felons was not what I was trained to do, I really wanted to help him.

"Hank," I began tentatively, "you've been in long enough to know what's right and what's wrong. You've been a good con here at Alcatraz and everyone likes and respects you. You got where your are in here by doing the right thing. It's not that hard to do the right thing and you know that. Well, it's the same on the outside. Sure, some things will be different out there than they were when you were arrested. But most things will still be the same. For one thing, there's a war going on, and that was the situation just before you went to jail. The things that are real are the same now as they were when you went to jail. You knew right from wrong then, and you know the difference now. Basically, Hank, all you'll have to do on the outside is what you've been doing in here. Work hard, keep your nose clean, and stay out of trouble."

"Thanks, Mr. Lageson. You make it sound pretty easy, but I'm not sure it will be. But thanks, thanks a lot."

The other inmates did their share to ease Hank's concerns, but they did it their way.

"Now, Hank, remember on the outside things are different. When you go into a store for a pack of smokes, you gotta pay for them. You can't just take 'em and walk away."

"Hey, Hank, you know when you get on the outside, you gotta do stuff on your own. There ain't gonna be any bells or whistles to tell you when to eat, go to work, or go to bed. You're totally on your own out there."

Hank accepted the kidding good-naturedly, for it was one of the happier phases of prison life. It was the time that one of their number was going home, and most cons who knew him were happy for him. So were the officers.

On another occasion, I was going to the city on one of my days off, and there happened to be a newly released inmate on the same boat. He was accompanied by the prison record clerk, whose duty it was to see that he boarded the correct train for his home. One of the other officers on the boat offered us all a lift into downtown San Francisco, and the discharged inmate accompanied us. During the entire ride down to Market Street, his eyes seemed to bulge from their sockets at the sights. Although he had seen many of these things in magazine photographs, viewing the real thing dazzled him. I recall his complete amazement at seeing an army Jeep speed out of the gates of Fort Mason, and he followed it with his gaze until it was out of sight. The record clerk informed me later that the inmate was so appreciative of the treatment he had received that he offered to purchase him a gift. The clerk naturally declined the offer, informing the lad that he'd need all of his twenty dollars release money for the expenses he'd incur in getting across the country to his home. Unfortunately, we heard later that this young man was back in jail within a few months of his release. His crime: armed robbery in the District of Columbia.

When inmates were to be discharged they were "dressed out" at the main gate. This involved them being dressed in a suit and tie in place of the convict denim they wore in prison. If the convict had a federal hold on him, federal marshals were always there to take him into custody. If a prisoner was to be delivered into the hands of state authorities, the arresting state officers were present to handcuff him as he came ashore at the Fort Mason pier. Despite the fact that an inmate was being discharged, it was always a tense time when he was being discharged into the custody of another law enforcement agency. But it was always a festive occasion when an inmate was being readied for discharge into the free world. The inmate to be released was always nervous, but the officers were jovial and helpful to the departing prisoner.

During one of these dressing out episodes, the departing convict turned over a five-dollar bill to the associate warden and informed him that he had received it from one of the officers. After the inmate was released, the officer was questioned regarding his action and given a reprimand. He was admonished that if he desired to give the inmate a gift, he should have gone through the proper channels to do so. The officer became quite upset over the reprimand and a violent argument followed, with much unpleasant name-calling. I was privy to the whole affair, a disturbing and unnecessary event. The final outcome was the resignation of the officer from the custodial staff. Most of us were sympathetic to the administration's position in the case, and could not relate to an officer who first, donated money to an outgoing inmate, and second, did it surreptitiously in violation of regulations.

Several weeks after one of the chains had left Alcatraz for transfer to another institution, we received word that two members of the group had broken free while being transported on a prison bus somewhere in the South. One of these inmates had been the garage mechanic on the dock during his years at Alcatraz, and had been a well-behaved convict. He was a braggart, however, and told tall tales of his notorious escapades while a free man. Most of the inmates and all of the officers ignored his stories.

Upon his return to Alcatraz after his brief stretch of freedom, he was derisively dubbed "Dillinger," and the inmates had plenty of laughs at his expense. One would have expected that his escape, while admittedly of limited duration, would have garnered respect, but that was not the case. Apparently, his history of big talk and self-aggrandizement had robbed him of his credibility and prevented his fellow inmates from taking him seriously, even when he did something noteworthy.

Undoubtedly, one of the most interesting and engaging of the so-called Alcatraz "big names" with whom I dealt with was the Count. He called himself Count Victor Lustig, and claimed to be of Czechoslovakian royalty. While I have no independent evidence regarding his title and lineage, his stories sounded convincing. It was accepted by everyone that the Count was not an American citizen, and was in the United States under a cloud as mysterious as his background. The unchallenged consensus among the convicts was that the Count was the quintessential con man, among the best in the world at what he did. He was the king of swindlers, cheaters, and deceivers. He preyed almost exclusively upon those with larceny in their hearts, who hoped to profit from one of the Count's nefarious schemes. The vast majority of his victims were just as dishonest as he was, but not nearly as clever.

The Count's file at Alcatraz listed him as Robert Miller, and he was serving only a four-year sentence. While he lacked the violent credentials of so many of his Alcatraz contemporaries, there was more to his criminal background than fraud. While being held in the federal detention headquarters in New York City, he managed to escape though a ventilator. He was soon recaptured, but his escape history, plus his alien status, made him a flight risk and a candidate for transfer to Alcatraz.

I met the Count when I worked as officer in charge of the mat shop, where he worked as the janitor. Being small and slight of build, he could not perform jobs requiring great strength or heavy physical exertion. Consequently, he was usually assigned chores as a janitor or low-level handyman. Lustig was a favorite of the inmates in large part because of his endless supply of stories about his criminal exploits before he went to prison. During smoke and rest breaks, he was constantly being asked to tell and retell his many tales.

One of the most requested stories dealt with the Count's experience in a brothel in Pittsburgh, Pennsylvania. It seems that he had swindled the leading madam of Pittsburgh, bilking her out of several thousands of dollars with one of his many schemes. Since she had no recourse through the legal system, she sought her revenge through the underworld, where she was very well connected.

"That old broad was really connected with the mob," the Count related, "and she was out to get me. Before I could get out of town, she had two of her heavy-duty mob customers get after me. A couple of really bad-ass torpedoes nailed me as I was packing to leave town, and hauled me to one of her whorehouses in this classy section of town. She was there to watch those two guys blow me away. I don't think she was even paying them. They was friends of hers, and after they blew my brains out they'd each get a girl for the night and that would be the end of the story and me.

"I had to act fast, and act fast I did. I admitted to taking her money fraudulently, but told her that killing me wouldn't get her money back. I was broke, I told her, and if her gunsels blew me away, all she'd have was a dead Czech that she'd have to get rid of. On the other hand, with my help, she could rip off one of her high-roller customers using the same scam she fell for. I'd help her set some guy up, and she'd get all her money back and then some. She fell for my plan, called off the torpedoes, and set us all up with girls for the evening. It was one of my better scams.

"The next day, the cops decided to stake out the place and arrest everyone coming out of there. When I saw that I told Ruby, 'Hey, I'm not leaving.' Since we were now partners, she was fine with that. 'Okay, Count,' she said, 'Stay 'til the heat cools down, but don't wear my girls out.'

"I tell you, it was the greatest four days of my life, great food, good booze, and all them pretty whores for free."

Another of the Count's schemes was one he labeled a legitimate operation. He noticed that many hotels did not have ink in the inkwells on the desks in their rooms. So, he obtained a secret ink recipe and began selling it to hotels on a door-to-door basis. In the meantime, he was negotiating with a large national hotel chain to supply them with all the ink they needed in the rooms. "But one of my partners double-crossed me and colluded with a nationally known ink company to steal the business. So I went back to swindling da dumb suckers."

The most sensational of all the Count's operations, however, was his "money machine." This device held appeal to those in the underworld, for it appeared to be an easy-to operate counterfeiting machine. "My money machine was a gadget which would turn out phony money for the guy who owned it. I would put a real twenty-dollar bill in the machine and explain to the sucker that, through a process which I had perfected, the print of the money would be made from the real bill to the paper which I put into the machine. We would turn out a couple of bills, and I would have the sucker take them to the bank and ask the teller to look it over. The teller would look at the bills and tell the sucker that they was good. Of course the bills was good, because there was a bunch of real bills in the machine. When the sucker was satisfied he would buy the machine and I was out of town. The sucker would make a bunch of bills and think he had something real good, but pretty soon the machine would run out of real bills. So what could the sucker do? He couldn't go to the police and have me arrested for selling him a phony counterfeiting machine. So he was out of luck unless he could sell the machine to somebody else. Like I said, I was a long way off by then."

The convicts loved the story and laughed hysterically. One of the group called out, "Hey, Count, tell the boss about the sheriff in Texas."

"Yeah, that's a pretty good one. While I was in jail in Texas waiting to be tried, on another caper, I sold a machine to the sheriff. He was a bigger crook than me, and I guess he did some time for it afterwards when he tried to sell the machine to some other sucker."

According to the numerous stories regarding the Count, he spared no one. Women were as legitimate to prey upon as men, and he used his glib tongue and manners to separate many a charmed matron from a portion of her wealth. A motion picture version of the Count's exploits was produced for television some years later, and many of the mat shop tales were brought to life on the screen. The money machine was just as funny on TV as the Count's version on The Rock.

During the escape attempt of 1946, the Count was caught in a difficult situation in the basement. He spent several hours trapped in the restroom, which came under tear gas attack from officers outside the cell house. He was finally rescued, but suffered lasting ill effects. Later, he developed a serious ear infection and was transferred to the hospital at Springfield, where he died only a short time before he was to be released. Thus ended the fantastic saga of one of the most clever of all thieves, yet one who proudly boasted that he never used a gun to take away a victim's money.

"Boss, I used my brains to separate the money from da suckers."

Thus went life on Alcatraz. At times the monotony became oppressive. At times there were violent eruptions with injury and death. Always in the air was an element of tension. But there were also the lighter moments, which eased the boredom and tension. Inmates came and went, but the institution remained "Rock" solid. It endured for nearly thirty years as one of the most unique societies in the world. Certainly it was the most fascinating environment to which my family and I were ever exposed. Life on The Rock was truly unforgettable.